THE SUCCESSFUL POLICE OFFICER

The Selection and Promotion of

THE SUCCESSFUL POLICE OFFICER

By

LAWRENCE R. O'LEARY, Ph.D.
Director of O'Leary, Brokaw, and Associates, Inc.
Associate Professor, Department of Psychology
University of Missouri at St. Louis

Edited by

R. Jerrad King

CHARLES C THOMAS · PUBLISHER
Springfield · Illinois · U.S.A.

Published and Distributed Throughout the World by
CHARLES C THOMAS • PUBLISHER
BANNERSTONE HOUSE
301-327 East Lawrence Avenue, Springfield, Illinois, U.S.A.

© *1979, by* CHARLES C THOMAS • PUBLISHER
ISBN 0-398-03805-8
Library of Congress Catalog Card Number: 78-5865

Printed in the United States of America

N-2

Library of Congress Cataloging in Publication Data

O'Leary, Lawrence R.
    The successful police officer

    Bibliography: p. 173.
    Includes index.
    1. Police—Recruiting.   2. Police—Personnel management.
3. Prediction of occupational success.
I. King, R. Jerrad.   II. Title.
HV7936.R5046   363.2'2   78-5865
ISBN 0-398-03805-8

This book is dedicated to my parents,
a tremendous influence in my life:
Catherine Mary Creane
and
Robert Emmett O'Leary.

FOREWORD

THE GREATEST asset any law enforcement organization has is the people it selects, assigns and promotes. Clearly, 80 to 85% of a law enforcement budget centers around the people within that organization. People accomplish goals.

People in law enforcement organizations define, articulate, and accomplish the goals of that particular organization. Without a concern for the human factor in organizations, few organizations could ever exist beyond a level of mediocrity. Who is selected for law enforcement becomes critical because the leaders of the future come from the selection process. Leaders in law enforcement must be selected from a professional and comprehensive base because of the organizational need for a few people to work with many people in accomplishing the goals of professional law enforcement.

The selection and promotion of a law enforcement officer is, in all probability, the most critical internal function of any agency.

In the past we have attempted to select and promote personnel on the basis of those accomplishments that were not necessarily germane to the perceived responsibility. In today's society it is even more important that the law enforcement organization strive to select and promote the most qualified people, for upon their shoulders lies the real future of professional law enforcement.

In this volume, Doctor O'Leary has laid out a step by step procedure which can be used in developing a job-related selection process, leading to the selection of the best people and promotion of the more qualified candidates. This, plus such features as a thorough glossary of terms in the selection field, makes this a practical book for managers in criminal justice organizations.

NORMAN E. POMRENKE
Director
Southern Police Institute

vii

INTRODUCTION

O UR SOCIETY is confronted with numerous challenges in today's world. Among these, the whole question of whether society can survive under the rule of law is one of the most basic.

For the past two hundred years, this country has conducted an experiment in human government which has generated some substantial successes and some significant failures. If the experiment is to continue and if civilization is to survive, a legal and judicial system of some sort must not only exist, but must also respond to the everchanging challenges of the society which it serves.

1. The increase in crime rate.
2. The limited involvement on the part of the public in crime prevention.
3. The difficulty of the judicial system in rapidly, efficiently, and justly disposing of court cases.
4. The difficulty of the penal system in discharging its objective of rehabilitating the criminal.
5. The difficulty of police organizations in effectively responding to law enforcement needs.

All of these are both causes and symptoms of a *law enforcement crisis* now facing this society.

This book deals with the last facet of this problem. I believe that the solution to the particular problem of police organizations cannot be achieved unless high caliber and competent individuals occupy decision-making positions within law enforcement agencies. As important as the entry level police officer is, significant change within law enforcement agencies will be very difficult without an enlightened group of influential decisionmakers in supervisory and administrative positions.

In order to address this problem meaningfully, the entire process by which a police officer is selected and later promoted must be examined. To look at one particular selection component (e.g. a promotion test) is a very narrow view of the problem. Although a review of each component is important, that review must be placed within the context of an examination of the entire selection and promotion system.

This book will examine the process whereby an individual deciding to enter the police force is selected and moved upward within the organization. Suggestions will be made as to how this can be done with a minimum number of errors and a resultant reduction in poor performance, which is a result of poor selection and placement.

This review process will involve examining past practices, not with the intent of pointing the finger at any particular process but with the intent of learning from past problems and building on these to establish a more effective, job-related, and valid assessment approach.

It is virtually impossible to develop a selection system which makes no errors. Consequently, the goal of the selection system is to minimize the number of errors associated with it.

The objective of a successful selection system should be clearly delineated because it can save much grief later on. If a personnel director is looking for perfection in the selection process and is prepared to abandon any selection tool that "allows mistakes," he will be condemned to a career of adopting and subsequently rejecting all possible selection tools.

Obviously, this would be an extremely frustrating experience. Hence the person in search of an optimum selection program should be prepared to say, "Yes, my selection system rejected someone who was capable, but it rejects few of those people and accepts fewer people who are not capable of doing the job than alternative selection approaches."

Most people are in favor of good selection systems in the law enforcement field because there is widespread agreement that the caliber of personnel drawn into this field is critically important. The police officer who is in the department because he likes to "break heads" is bad for society and for the department. Equally damaging is the sergeant who cannot lead, make decisions, or plan and organize his work and that of his patrol.

The basic issue is how do we obtain the best selection system. More specifically, how does this department go about systematically developing a selection system which is job related and effectively minimizes errors in selection. The system must also satisfy the many legal pressures being put on police departments today.

Psychologists have been in the business of testing for a long time, and they have had a number of successes as well as some notable failures in this area. However, one indisputable fact is that *a successful selection system must begin with a thorough knowledge of the position for which the department is selecting*.

It makes no sense at all to try to develop one kind of selection device or predictor* for all the jobs in a particular department. Before you can develop a successful selection system, you *must* have a clear understanding of all the tasks performed by the people in that particular job. This should be specific to a given department.

One should not *assume* that a test which is successful for the selection of sergeants in the Los Angeles Police Department will necessarily be successful for the same position in the Kansas City Police Department or the Rochester Police Department. While certain responsibilities may be common for these positions in all the departments, there are numerous duties and responsibilities which are department-specific, thereby rendering the positions distinct in many ways.

---

*A predictor is anything which can be reliably and consistently measured prior to the selection decision, e.g. test score, interview, background information, physical fitness results, etc.

ACKNOWLEDGMENTS

I would like to express my particular gratitude for my wife Gerty's encouragement in the effort necessary to write the book. I would further thank Robert Shoop for his critical remarks, as well as Jeanne Boesing and Anne Gavin for their skill and patience in typing this manuscript and its many revisions.

L.R.O'L.

CONTENTS

THE SUCCESSFUL POLICE OFFICER

Chapter 1

WHAT ARE YOU REALLY TRYING TO ACCOMPLISH?

"ALL YOU have to do is look at some of the people who are being hired and promoted in modern police departments, and you know something is wrong." This comment was made by a sergeant in a medium-sized police department. While there are many excellent police personnel being selected and promoted by the old system, there is a growing awareness that the percentage of errors must be reduced. The solution to this problem is found in the concept explained in the introduction: (1) identify what qualities you are looking for and then (2) develop a systematic method of measuring those qualities.

Procedures in different departments vary greatly, but a common thread usually runs through their selection systems. There are two types of selection procedures in most departments: one for the entry level position (e.g. police officer, cadet, and trooper) and another for promotional decisions. Usually the candidate for the entry level position is given a reference check, then an eyesight examination, followed by a written test of general intelligence. This in turn leads the candidate to a test of physical fitness, after which he undergoes a medical examination and finally, a psychiatric test and an oral board.

On the surface, there is nothing wrong with this system. The problem lies in its implementation. In most police departments there is a great deal of uncertainty on the part of the interviewers, the test developers, and others as to what *exactly* they are looking for in this candidate.

In many instances, interviewers have some vague notion about their purpose in the selection system but nothing more. As a

Author's note: Throughout this volume the pronoun "he" is presented generically to represent a member of either sex. The publisher believed such a presentation would serve both consistency and brevity.

result, they go into the interview unprepared and plan to "chat" with the candidate for a while and "get a gut feeling" about his qualifications for the job. This problem is usually complicated by the fact that many interviewers for police departments receive no training prior to the interviewing. Thus, they often waste the little time available by asking questions which yield a minimum of information.

Two of the most common mistakes of the untrained interviewer are (1) asking questions which yield very little information and (2) seeking information which is already available through the application. For example, one interviewer may consistently ask the candidate, "Did you like your last job?" The answer to this question tells the interviewer very little. If the candidate says no, he either believes that the interviewer wants him to say no or else he did not enjoy his previous job. In either event, the interviewer does not know which is really true.

Another problem with the above system is that the untrained interviewers are usually on a tight schedule and have a maximum of twenty minutes in which to chat with each candidate. This time frame is very brief and frequently involves questions which were answered on the application form which the interviewer had not previously reviewed.

The alternative is to develop a somewhat structured interview with trained interviewers who are familiar with (1) the qualities desired in a police officer and (2) the types of questions which will elicit information relevant to determining whether the candidate possesses these qualities.

The measure of general intelligence is all too often graded in an arbitrary manner, such as "We can't even consider anyone for a police position who has less than an IQ of 110." The intention behind this kind of decision is well-meaning. Police officers have a very difficult job trying to meet the responsibilities of their position, and it does require a certain amount of intelligence to perform those duties.

The fact of the matter is that there are many very bright people who have an IQ of less than 110. Over the years, the author has taught at a number of universities and has, on occasion, had the opportunity to see the IQ scores of some of his students. On a couple of occasions, students who obtained very high marks in school were at or below the 110 IQ figure.

The point is that an arbitrary cut-off in this field of general intelligence can deselect qualified persons. This problem is further complicated by the cultural bias written into many "paper and pencil tests" of intelligence. This topic will be discussed later in this book.

Federal legislation such as Title VII of the 1964 Civil Rights Act and the 1972 Amended Civil Rights Act has dramatically affected the amount of attention given selection and promotional programs by both private and public employers. The basic thrust of this legislation is to obtain a selection procedure which identifies the best person for the job, based on merit.

However, the practical implementation of the law through such agencies as the Equal Employment Opportunity Commission (EEOC) and the Office of Federal Contracts Compliance Programs (OFCCP) has led to some legitimate disagreements and issues, some of which the Supreme Court has dealt with (*Griggs v. Duke Power Company*, 420 E2d 1225 and *Moody v. Albemarle* 271 F. Sup. 27) and some which it had sidestepped (*Defunis v. Odegaard*, 416 U.S. 312). Whatever the legitimacy of the arguments on both sides, the impact of this federal legislation has led to examination of police department selection systems in order to identify any "adverse impact" existent within the system.

Adverse impact occurs when a greater percentage of minorities are rejected by the selection system than nonminorities. The Federal Executive Agency guidelines define adverse impact as occurring when "A selection rate for any racial, ethnic, or sex group becomes less than four-fifths ($4/5$) or 80 percent of the rate for the group with the highest rate." (Department of Justice, Department of Labor, and Civil Service Employee Selection Guidelines). When such an adverse impact exists, the employer is required to demonstrate that his selection system is valid. Either he must prove statistically that people who score higher on his selection program also do better on the job (criterion-related validity) or demonstrate that his selection system involves actual parts of the job or simulations of the job (content validity—having a candidate for a keypunch job operate a keypunch machine and turn out so many cards in a given time).

In addition to the problem of little time being devoted to the selection procedure and potential cultural bias, there is the very real problem of identifying what the job is and what knowledges, skills, abilities, and personal characteristics (referred to as KSAPCs) are desired for the position.

Before a selection system is developed, the objective of the system should be *clearly defined*. If it is poorly defined and there is not more than a vague notion of the objectives, there is a high probability that the selection system will be a failure. Some systematic analysis of the job for which the selection system is being developed must be conducted for the purpose of identifying the specific KSAPCs required for the position. Without that list, developing a selection system is like shooting craps—you may luck out but the odds are against you.

A related problem is that many police organizations either have no existing job analysis data or their job descriptions are not sufficiently specific to provide a sound list of measurable KSAPCs.

A fourth problem can be defined as the "crush of bodies" problem. One example will serve to illustrate this point. Recently, the New York State Highway Patrol received about 30,000 applications for some 120 entry-level positions. The problem develops when the agency with a limited selection budget attempts to give everyone a fair chance at being considered for the position.

Although this is not always true, predictors with a high degree of validity are usually more expensive than predictors which are less valid. It is relatively inexpensive to administer a paper and pencil test to a large group of people. In many instances this selection system is less valid than a job simulation technique (e.g. an assessment center). The latter, however, is more expensive.

A fifth problem with current selection procedures is a reluctance to change brought about by the lack of autonomy in some police departments. In numerous cities and states, the department comes under the auspices of the civil service commission. In some instances, these authorities are reluctant to deviate from more traditional methods of selection. This is understandable from the perspective of people in the civil service system. They have seen paper and pencil tests deliver them from the spoils system. However, it is unfortunate that they are slow to change and view the selection process as something more than simply a paper and pencil test.

A sixth issue is sometimes referred to as job relatedness. Many departments have had the experience of watching candidates leave the written test or oral board shaking their heads in frustration because the test was not related to the position they were being tested for.

The job relatedness of a selection module or predictor is important for two reasons: (1) it is more likely to be valid (measure and predict success) and (2) it is more likely to generate some type of legal action if it does not relate to the job in question.

In one case, the author worked with a fire district in which a Wonderlic test of intelligence was administered to generate an eligibility list for promotion to fire captain. This test had very little to do with the duties of a fire captain. Many fire fighters spend a great deal of time in the firehouse pouring over technical books in preparation for promotional exams which they anticipate will cover technical matters. Frustration from taking a test of general intelligence after studying for several months was exhibited in one instance in which fire captain candidates came back to the firehouse from the test and began throwing all their technical books down the stairs in an act of hostility and frustration. This test had little apparent job relatedness.

The seventh problem is probably the most important. It deals with the validity of the particular test including the oral board being used. The concept of validity will be explored and thoroughly discussed in a later chapter. It is enough to say at this point that a predictor is valid if people who score high on the predictor also score high on job performance. As mentioned earlier, there are many cases in which the people who scored high on the oral boards or on the written test performed far less favorably on the job than their scores would indicate.

There are certainly other problems that a particular department will face which have not been mentioned here. The person making a decision about his organization's selection systems has numerous considerations to keep in mind. Under such circumstances, one must remember the basic point underlying all these considerations: *the importance of the selection system being related to the job and, therefore, being valid.*

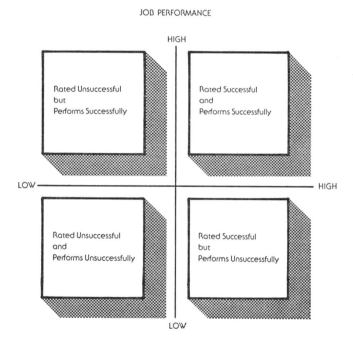

JOB PERFORMANCE

HIGH

Rated Unsuccessful
but
Performs Successfully

Rated Successful
and
Performs Successfully

LOW ——————————————————— HIGH

Rated Unsuccessful
and
Performs Unsuccessfully

Rated Successful
but
Performs Unsuccessfully

LOW

ALTERNATIVE OUTCOMES OF ANY SELECTION SYSTEM

Figure 1.

The alternatives in quadrants 1 and 3 are misses, because how the applicant is rated by the selection system is at variance with how he performs after being hired. Obviously the diagram oversimplifies the evaluation of a job incumbent since there are degrees of success. However, the diagram is illustrative only. One might think of putting a person in a successful category if after a year on the job one can say that the person would be hired again, given the chance to remake such a decision.

By way of review, we have examined a number of problems that currently exist with selection systems in the police field. They are the following:

1. Poorly defined KSAPCs for the position under consideration.
2. Poorly trained and poorly informed interviewers.
3. A misdirected confidence in the effective selection capabilities of such paper and pencil tests as IQ tests.
4. The "crush of bodies" problem.
5. Adverse impact.
6. Local control of selection systems.
7. Lack of job relatedness of the selection system's components.

With these problems in view, there is little wonder that many police department administrations consider personnel selection as one of their principal problem areas. As a result, there is an enormous expenditure of time and energy in the attempt to comply with objectives which often are conflicting and criticisms which, though deserved, fail to account for the complicated nature of this problem.

A personnel specialist within the police field quickly concludes that he cannot please everyone. By definition, any selection system will deselect or eliminate a substantial number of people. If it does not, then it is not effective and is not meeting its objectives. It is natural that those who are deselected will have reservations about the appropriateness or accuracy of the selection system.

Second, as was pointed out earlier, any selection system will make errors and these will draw the attention of the system's critics. Being aware of these realities is important because the personnel analyst can destroy the credibility of the selection process in the quixotic search for the perfect selection system (which does not exist). Instead, the selector must be satisfied to state that "the selection system that this department uses is as job related and valid as we can make it." That is what this book is all about—enabling the personnel departments in the law enforcement field to make the above statement.

Chapter 2

WHAT ARE YOU TRYING TO PREDICT?

THE OBJECTIVE of any selection system is to *predict* success on the job. Therefore, the first step in the development of such a process is to *identify specifically what you are trying to measure.* As one deputy chief of police told me, "Developing a selection system on the basis of a poor job analysis is like building a beautiful ship that has a flimsy keel and hull underwater." This is an effective analogy because developing a selection system to measure success when one is not clear what "success" is will be doomed to failure.

If this is so obvious, why does it have to be stated specifically? Frankly, this is a perplexing question. When the statement is made that "you must know what you are trying to measure in order to have a successful selection system," everyone nods their heads in agreement. It makes good sense and generates very little argument. Yet, despite this consensus, experience shows that a large number of selection systems fail because they do not meet this principle of job selection.

One possible reason is that there is no one method of analyzing jobs which excels over all other methods. There are numerous methods which are equally effective. Perhaps this leads to the feeling that one simply needs to get some broad ideas about the necessary knowledges, skills, and abilities for the job.

Another reason may be an eagerness to get on with the "important aspects" of the selection system, such as picking tests, establishing qualifications, and developing some kind of job performance measure for subsequent validity studies. We will discuss all these steps later in this book. However, the reader should not lose sight of the fact that the process of identifying the necessary knowledges, skills, and abilities for a specific target position is an essential element in developing a valid selection system.

The objective of this first component, the job analysis, is to develop a specific list of the necessary knowledges, skills, and abilities (KSAs) required by the job. The analysis should indicate which of these KSAs are more important than others and which one needs "at entry" into the position. If the person is not required to have the KSA at entry and can be taught that skill (i.e. the skill in making an arrest), then logically this is something that should not be a criteria for selection.

While there are a variety of job analysis techniques, there are two broad categories which are widely used. These include the element approach (Ernest Primoff, 1974) and the task analysis approach such as the one used by the United States Department of Labor (1972). As these two methods are discussed, one major division of the task analysis approach is a rather specific approach known as the "critical incident" technique (J.C. Flanagan, 1953). There are two other techniques such as Ernest McCormick's position analysis questionnaire (1969). Those who are interested in these options are referred to the above references.

Sample Job Analysis Procedure

The American Psychological Association's *Standards for Educational and Psychological Tests* (1974) clearly delineates the information needed from a job analysis. These include specific information on the KSAs required for the position and the level of each KSA required. This type of information should also be accompanied by the relative importance of each KSA for the successful performance of the position in question.

Any of the approaches mentioned above is acceptable as part of an accurate job analysis. One procedure which is a direct descendent of the task analysis approach has been developed and used successfully in the state of Iowa. It has been applied to police positions and many other public employee positions (McCarthy et al, 1977).

This procedure is very detailed and specific but it functions generally in the following manner. After the analyst has become familiar with the position to be analyzed (target position), he arranges a group meeting with a number of incumbents and supervisors of the target position. He then distributes a list of task statements which describe a substantial part of the duties of the target position. The incumbents and supervisors then attempt to improve on each task statement.

The statements must follow a specific format, thereby standardizing the material obtained. Here the administrator must be as explicit, clear, and direct as possible. For example, such statements as "reviews a subordinate's work" are deleted and reworded so that they are understood by anyone reading the statement. The statement "reviews a subordinate's work" is so general that ten people reading it could have ten different ideas of what specific tasks are being accomplished. In some cases, these types of phrases are unavoidable, but every effort is made to limit their use.

Once the group has completed the list of task statements, they are then asked to rank these tasks in terms of importance to success on the job. This is accomplished by rating the importance of each on a five-point scale, from unimportant to very important.

Then the administrator brings the group together to develop a list of the necessary KSAs to perform these tasks. It should be pointed out that the incumbents and supervisors of the target position should develop these tasks and KSAs since no one knows the job better than they do. It should be further emphasized that this action of taking incumbents and supervisors away from their work might create some grumbles about "getting on with the job," but usually they are pleased to be asked to help. After all, they are the people who will have to work with the products of the selection so in essence it is *their* procedure. As one bureau commander said, "This is the first time that I have ever been asked by any selection consultant what it takes to be a good detective in my department, and I've been a commander for many years."

The final step in the Iowa procedure involves the incumbents again meeting with the supervisor to identify the appropriateness of the selection system components. Here they indicate what qualifications they think are appropriate for the job, as they have previously indicated what KSAs are necessary for entry into the position.

They now review such things as test items and other components of the selection procedure and indicate on a rating scale how appropriate they are for the selection.

The Iowa procedure's principal advantage is its documented and systematic approach to job analysis. The procedure also involves each incumbent completing the information mentioned in a booklet which has a place for him to list background and years of work in the position in question and related fields. This material serves as a documentation for the accuracy and appropriateness of the job analysis data. This is important in verifying the authenticity of the job analysis data by establishing the credentials of the people who produce the information.

The objective of a job analysis, when preparing for the development of a selection procedure, is to provide the organization with the *specific* KSAs that are important for performance of the duties of the target position. Consequently, job analyses undertaken for other reasons, such as the establishment of pay classifications, may not be appropriate material for developing a selection system since they do not adequately specify the KSAs which are important.

Job descriptions in the files of many law enforcement organizations are probably a good starting point for sound job analysis. However, many job descriptions contain only vague references to required KSAs. Obviously, unless management has a clear picture of what it is trying to predict with its selection system, the system's effectiveness will be seriously jeopardized.

The effort put forth at this step of developing a selection system is critical because it is the *foundation* for what will come later. A job analysis is always important for developing a valid selection system. It has become even more important with the realization that certain test validation procedures are more acceptable to the court and some federal regulatory agencies than they had been in the past.

Now that a few comments have been made regarding the nature of job analyses, I would like to point out that few things appear less important to most practitioners than a job analysis. However, the fact is that a sound job analysis is essential and the foundation for an effective selection system.

A job analysis is not synonymous with the document usually called a job description. The latter is a paragraph or two or three which describes the major duties of the person in narrative form. It then may go on to list critical skills, minimum qualifications, and reporting responsibility. In contrast, a job analysis is a procedure which results in the generation of knowledges, skills, and abilities that are important to perform the position in question.

As mentioned before, there are no absolute best methods for determining the knowledges, skills, and abilities. One may select the diary method of having an incumbent or series of incumbents keep a diary or log of their activities or the critical incident method of having incumbents list specific behaviors that characterize good performance or characterize distinctly poor performance on the job or the task analysis method which depends on a number of things including the nature of the job. For example, one method involves actual job observation. In this method, the job analyst would observe the incumbent performing his duties. I was once asked on the witness stand while serving as an expert witness why I did not use the observation method of job analysis for the position of fire chief. In point of fact, I did observe the chief perform some of his duties. However, much of what a fire chief of a large metropolitan city does is inside his head: He makes decisions; he plans and organizes; he communicates with people on the phone, etc. Many of these activities are very difficult to get at clearly using the observation method. For this position, I selected a job analysis method which enabled me to get inside the chief's head by having him and his subordinates describe his duties and responsibilities as well as the major tasks he performs.

In the law enforcement field, the observation method is quite useful, particularly when a non–law-enforcement person or civilian is performing the job analysis. However, I typically use this as a supplement to the major job analysis approach that I use which is the traditional task analysis approach. Before getting into the specific steps of this task analysis method, and I believe it is important to do so because of the centrality of job analysis to sound selection procedures, I would like to stop for a minute and ask the question, "Why do a job analysis?"

A job analysis can accomplish three basic objectives. The first has been discussed to some extent and can best be articulated by the simple statement that successful prediction of who will do a good job necessitates that those developing the predictor system know what they are trying to predict. The second point or benefit to be derived from a job analysis is that the entire job will be thoroughly covered. In many job analysis activities I have talked with incumbents who have said, "Oh, this is important for the job but you can't test for it so I won't mention it." It is my suspicion that many knowledges, skills, and abilities have not been brought into play and listed as part of the job because someone thought that quality could not be measured. Other reasons for pieces of the job not being brought up include such things as "they are not really activities but the absence of activities." The police officer must spend large amounts of his time in the patrol car observing the situation around him as he patrols his sector. In one sense, he is performing a duty but in another sense he is really challenged by the boredom and the routine. This "lack of activity" is a real part of the job and in and of itself a task that is frequently not brought up. A thorough job analysis will get this down on paper to be included as part of the job and perhaps as even part of the selection system. Certainly, it will not be included as part of the selection system if it is not even mentioned.

The final benefit of a job analysis is that it "reduces the mystique" of the selection system and increases the acceptance of the system by the department. I have been familiar with a number of departments where the rank and file of the police organization are not privy to the basis on which promotion decisions (primarily) are made. With a thorough job analysis and a subsequent selection plan, the selection system can be developed and reviewed by anyone (e.g. incumbents, candidate's supervisors, federal agency representatives). Everything is aboveboard. It does not mean that you give everybody a copy of the test. It does mean that rational adults have an overall guideline of how the selection system is put together and how the promotion decisions are made.

One of the biggest issues that nonpersonnel people bring up about job analyses is "the necessity for all this nit-picking." As you will see in the job analysis, specific task statements are listed. There is one task statement for every separate and major responsibility of the target position being analyzed. Numbers of task statements can typically run anywhere from seven to twenty per job. Each task statement is written in a format which includes five elements: (1) Who is doing the action? (2) What is the action? (3) To whom/what is the action directed? (4) Why is the action being done? (5) How is the action done?

The question frequently arises because the nonpersonnel supervisor and even sometimes people in personnel and testing have difficulty understanding why such a specific format must be used and such care taken with every sentence or task statement written. Not only must each task statement be in a certain format but a number of words such as "oversees," "supervises," and "reviews" are to be avoided because they are misleading and can mean a thousand different things.

The answer to the question is very simply that a successful list of task statements from which the knowledges, skills, and abilities are generated must minimize the amount of misinterpretation. One way to tell if a task statement is adequate is to have a number of people independently read the statement and then describe the mental picture that they obtain from that statement. If each mental picture is somewhat similar to the others described, the task statement is an accurate one. This is particularly true if the descriptions are fairly specific. If the task statement is poorly written, there will be a lack of specificity in the mental pictures described and the statement will lack crispness and exactness. That exactness is the hallmark of a good task statement. That is why examples are freely used in parentheses within task statements, to contribute to this *specific* quality of the statement. Those who want to delve more thoroughly into this area and get into the specifics of how to conduct one proven approach to the critical facet of developing a sound selection system, which is job analyses, are referred to McCarthy et al (1977).

In conclusion, it is important to emphasize that *"A properly completed and thorough job analysis is as essential for the development of a sound selection system as electricity is for the use of a light bulb."*

Chapter 3

SELECTION, TESTING, AND TEST EVALUATION

THERE HAS been a great deal written about test validation, adverse impact, and many other facets of contemporary selection systems. Under these circumstances, it is easy to forget some basic and simple facts. We must keep in mind that the first objective of a selection system is to maximize accurate selection decisions and minimize inaccurate ones (see Figure 1).

Typically this is done by a systematic approach of identifying the job-related KSAs and subsequently developing methods for measuring as many of those KSAs as possible.

These measuring devices are called selection components. A selector is simply a measuring instrument used prior to making the final selection decision. Selectors are such things as paper and pencil tests, interviews, service ratings, physical fitness tests, and perhaps experience and training schools.

Because a single selector, such as a paper and pencil test of some form of technical knowledge (i.e. knowledge of city ordinances), measures only one facet of job success, there has been an emphasis on using a *systems approach* to selection. This approach simply suggests that if management is going to predict success on the job, they avoid hiring people on the basis of one facet of a multifaceted job. Consequently, law enforcement organizations are encouraged to identify what predictors can be used in the selection system and to combine these so as to account for all of the varied KSAs necessary for success on the job.

In day to day operations within the law enforcement field, one can readily see the price an organization pays for ignoring the selection system approach. Take, for example, an organization that would promote patrol officers to the position of sergeant on the basis of their knowledge of city ordinances. Such knowledge may be very important for success in that position, however, if

17

this were the sole predictor, the organization could easily wind up with ineffective leaders, administrators, planners, organizers, etc., *all of whom have a substantial knowledge of city ordinances.*

Validity

The term validity in the testing field means the capacity of a predictor or a series of predictors to actually measure what it claims to measure. If a mechanical comprehension test claims to measure a person's capacity to run a screw machine in an assembly plant, it is valid if persons scoring well on the test perform successfully in operating the screw machine.

An oral board is valid if it measures what it claims to measure. All too frequently an oral board is placed in the selection system with little attempt to delineate what the oral board can measure.

Hopefully, you can see that validity is closely tied to the concepts of a selector and what the specific instrument or selector system claims to measure. There are a number of ways a selector or a selector system can be established as valid. The first of these is called content validity.

The publication which contains the best description of standards for current testing practices is the *Standards for Educational and Psychological Tests* (1974). It has been prepared by a joint committee of the American Psychological Association, the American Educational Research Association, and the National Council on Measurement in Education. The booklet is seventy-six pages long and deals with such topics as validity, reliability, tests, manuals, reports, and the use of tests. The chapters outside of those on reliability and validity can be read by the layman with little problem. Every user of tests in the law enforcement field should purchase a copy and have it as a ready reference in making decisions about test usage.

Content Validity

Given the ever increasing sophistication of personnel workers, many people should be able to understand the chapter on reliability and validity as well. One other reason for having this publication readily available is the substantial credence given to its contents by courts of law in test discrimination cases. "Evidence of content validity is required when the test user wishes to estimate how an individual performs in the universe of situations the test is intended to represent." (*American Psychological Association, 1974*).

One can consider choosing content validity as the proper model in a selection system for a given position when the test or other component of the selection system consists of "pieces of the job." For example, typing tests would be "content valid" for a position in which typing was a substantial part of the job itself (e.g. typist clerk). The same could be true for many job simulation exercises which require the applicant to demonstrate efficiency on a specific task which is contained in the job itself.

This is why a typing test for a secretarial position is a valid test only if the job involves a good deal of typing. The test is a "piece of the job." The same thing can be said for shorthand, keypunch operating, or even driving a forklift truck. If it is a substantial part of the position and there is no basic training program associated with the job, then parts of the job can be used as a valid part of the selection system.

Criterion-Related Validity

A second type of validity, criterion-related validity, involves the quantitative measuring of job performance (e.g. the officer's rating of his job performance, number of arrests, number of citizens' complaints filed against an officer, days late for roll call). This measure is called a criterion, and as the reader can see, one has to be rather selective in choosing a criterion or a series of criteria. For example, the criterion of citizens' complaints may be questionable in certain neighborhoods because it assumes that "sound police performance is characterized by a minimum of citizens' complaints." I had one police captain tell me that the officers who have no complaints against them in a tough neighborhood are avoiding these complaints by playing it safe and not really doing their job.

The same can be said about other criteria. However, once a criterion can be agreed upon, quantitative measures on the criterion are collected for a group of incumbents in one job (e.g. sergeant). These criteria measures are correlated (a simple statistical procedure) with one or more predictor scores (e.g. tests, physical fitness, education). If people who perform high on the predictor also perform high on the criterion, the correlation will be statistically significant and the predictor is judged to have "criterion validity." There are numerous considerations that have to be dealt with in this process of generating criterion validity but we will discuss those later. The objective here is simply to understand the concept of criterion validity.

Construct Validity

Content– and criterion-related validity are the two most prominent types of validation found in studies on organizational selection systems. A third type of validation which is less frequently used, but is also legitimate, is "construct validity." This type of validation is very involved and requires numerous studies. It attempts to measure internal constructs or qualities frequently assessed by personality tests. One example of such a construct in the law enforcement field would be "pressure on the street." One might try to measure a person's ability to work under such pressure and measure that construct from a number of different predictors (e.g. a stress interview or situational stress introduced in the police academy). Construct validity is usually established by a series of validity studies measuring the construct from different perspectives and developing a whole theory explaining on-job behavior. (For further discussion of construct validity, see the *Standards for Educational and Psychological Tests,* 1974.)

There are other types of validity, such as face validity which is of little value in assisting people who are interested in predicting job success because it simply reflects the "apparent validity of the selection device."

There are a number of reasons for the appeal of content validity. First, there is a great deal of logic to using the job itself or pieces of the job to predict who will be successful on it. Second, it does not require a great deal of sophisticated statistical analysis. Third, content validity does not require a large number of people who have taken the test and whose performance has been measured on the job (as in criterion-related validity) in order to establish the existence of validity.

How does one establish content validity? By demonstrating the similarity between the content of the selector system (e.g. the typing test) and the content of the job itself (e.g. typing responsibilities). This is typically done *through a thorough job analysis* which emphasizes the "how" aspect of the task statements. As the incumbents describe the specific methods in which the tasks are performed, the job analyst is able to examine these parts of the task statements to use as methods for developing valid predictors for the position.

The disadvantage of content validity is conversely the principal strength of criterion-related validity. That is, the content validity does not develop, or at least has not developed, as much quantitative data or "scores" which can be statistically tested for significance, as the criterion model has. (However this is changing slightly, see Lawshe, 1975.) On the other hand, criterion-related validity is based on the relationship between test results and some measure of actual performance on the job by past applicants. Such data allows for a statistical procedure known as correlation which results in a number, the significance of which can be put to a statistical test. This statistical test is considered an advantage of criterion-related validity because it appears to be more scientific and quantifiable by answering the question "Does performance on the predictor(s) actually identify which candidates will be successful on the job?" These concepts will be further discussed in a subsequent chapter on quantification but the advantages of the two approaches are discussed here briefly for orientation purposes.

It should be pointed out that validity of a test is a necessary characteristic of a successful selection system. Another necessary characteristic is reliability, which refers to the consistency of the scores earned on a selection system. To be more specific, if a person gets a score of 60 on a scale of 100 on Tuesday and comes back on Friday and gets a score of 95, then the test's reliability is low (i.e. it is inconsistent) and, therefore, of little value. If you have an unreliable predictor (it does not have to give similar scores on the same people) it cannot be a valid predictor.

For example, I was asked to go bowling with my brother-in-law who is an avid bowler. I bowl very seldom and, as a result, very inconsistently. On this particular Saturday afternoon, after not having bowled for two and one-half years, I managed a score of 185. My brother-in-law was convinced that he had been hustled; but, in actuality, the score and the single performance was an inaccurate indicator of my bowling skills. It was inaccurate because it was unreliable. This could have been indicated if I had been asked to bowl two or three additional games in which case my average probably would have been lower than 185. This inconsistency of performance is what is referred to in measuring jargon as unreliability. It is the same thing that happens when a particular baseball player goes four for four at the plate on a given day, but over the entire season he may only compile a .200 average. As a result of this close relationship between validity and reliability, it has been determined that the validity coefficient can be no greater than the square root of the reliability coefficient (to be discussed later).

Reliability and Standardization

Another quality of importance to a selector system is objectivity, which refers to the probability that the selector will be scored the same when evaluated independently by two people. Standardization is the final quality of a successful selection system. This quality simply refers to the fact that the predictor components are administered under standardized conditions. A predictor system is not going to work properly if some applicants are given eighty minutes and others only forty minutes. These concepts will be further described later in the book.

In closing this section, two basic concepts should be emphasized. First, validity is at the heart of a successful selection system. If the selector system or a specific component of that system does not predict job success or contribute to such a prediction, then it is not doing its job. It is invalid.

The second point to be emphasized is the importance of using a systems approach to selection. Success in the law enforcement field at any level is usually not due to one single factor. The *Standards for Educational and Psychological Tests* (1974) explicitly and succintly affirms this idea in standard H2, "A test user should consider more than one variable for assessment and the assessment of any given variable by more than one method." (For most purposes, the evaluation of a person requires description that is both broad and precise; a single assessment or assessment procedure rarely provides all relevant facets of a description.)

Decisions about individuals should ordinarily be based on assessment of more than one dimension; when feasible, all major dimensions related to the outcome of the decision should be assessed and validated. This is the principle of multivariate prediction; where individual predictors have some validity and relatively low intercorrelations, the composite is usually more valid than prediction based on a single variable. It is not always possible to conduct the empirical validation study (certainly not in working with problems of individuals one at a time), but the principle can be observed.

In any case, care should be taken that assessment procedures focus on important characteristics; decisions are too often based on assessment of only those dimensions that can be conveniently measured with known validity.

I have had officers and police administrators at times say *this* is the key factor or *that* is the basic component required for a successful patrol officer or a successful detective. There is some truth to these statements but the people making them were emphasizing the importance of a basic quality, and one should not conclude that a candidate with that particular quality (such as ambition or drive or dedication to work) does not need anything else. Imagine, if you will, an extreme case in which the candidate is highly dedicated to the law enforcement field but cannot speak English. This extreme example is given to emphasize the point that the evaluation of a candidate for a specific position should evaluate the total candidate in terms of the knowledges, skills, abilities, and personal characteristics (KSAPCs) necessary for the job. *The basic point here is that such an evaluation, in order to be job related and thorough, should involve a total selection systems approach in developing valid components.*

There is a major difference, which is frequently obscured, between the ordinary perception of "testing" and selection. Selection refers to the entire process identifying a related number of candidates from among a larger group who will be placed into a promotional or entry level position on a permanent basis. More specifically, selection involves an entire system which begins with the identification of the knowledges, skills, and abilities which are important to the job and ends with the placing of the identified candidate in a permanent position with the department. That system may involve something such as the following:

(1) Job analysis of the sergeant position → (2) recruiting effort →

(3) test → (4) oral board → (5) working test (probation period) →

(6) permanent position

This is the usual selection system applied in many police departments, although the working test period is not frequently associated as part of the selection. A great deal more will be said about this latter part, suffice to say that one of the best predictors of future performance is present performance in that job. As such, the actual job itself can be a very powerful predictor of what the person will do in the future.

In contrast to this rather involved selection process, the ordinary perception of testing refers specifically to some form of paper and pencil test (the EEOC guidelines on selection define tests in a much broader sense than this ordinary perception). Testing is one component of selection. Throughout this book the author will be referring to a selection system and selection components of that system. This is consistent with the fact that successful performance in any job, and certainly those within the law enforcement field, is not a matter of one's knowledge in a certain area or one's specific ability but a *complex network of knowledge, skills, and abilities which require measurement from a number of different areas (components) to generate a valid selection component score.*

Let us now get into the concept of validity in a little more detail. We have already discussed the existence of a number of types of validity (American Psychological Association, 1974). As you will recall, the statistical demonstration of validity which is most commonly used is that of some form of criterion-related validity. Believe it or not, we have already computed a number of *validity coefficients.*

A validity coefficient is no more than a correlation coefficient between a predictor score and some measure of performance. In the previous chapter, the correlation between performance on the test and performance on the job was in effect a validity coefficient. It is an expression of the degrees of the relationship between the predictor and the job performance (criterion) variable.

Basically there are two types of criterion-related validity. The first type is the more desirable but the less frequently used of the two. It is called *predictive validity,* and involves a correlation of predictor scores at point A in time with some measure of job performance (e.g. supervisor ratings), point B, at which time some performance measures are correlated. The two sets of scores are then correlated to yield a predictive validity coefficient.

If I want to do a predictive validity study between a set of sergeant's promotional test scores and job performance measures, I cannot use that test score to decide which sergeants go into the job. For a predictive validity coefficient to occur, selection of the candidates cannot be based on the predictors subsequently used in the predictor validity study. I must use some other basis for making that decision. This is why the predictive validity approach is rarely used. It frequently calls for administration of some predictor such as the paper and pencil test with the commitment to avoid using two test scores to make a decision. Departments do not usually administer tests and then not use them.

The reason for this strange requirement is the need to generate something we saw before as a very useful part of a predictor— namely, a large variance of scores. *If you use a predictor to select people, by necessity you are going to be reducing variance in the scores because you are going to eliminate low scoring people on the predictor.* For example, if I administer a paper and pencil test for sergeant and make the decision that fifty is my cutoff point on the test, all those people who score below fifty will not get a chance to try the job nor get any kind of performance measure established because they will not be promoted. From a statistical standpoint, this presents a problem known as *restriction of range.*

The other type of criterion-related validity is called concurrent validity. It is the more common of the criterion validity studies and is computed by correlating predictor and performance measures collected concurrently. For example, administering a test to your current group of sergeants on whom you can also collect some type of performance measure allows for correlation to determine the strength of the relationship between test results and actual performance—thus, "concurrent validity."

Obviously, such a procedure can be harmed by restriction of range since the group of sergeants are a restricted group of people who have passed the police officer's test and subsequently the sergeant's test.

The other types of validity have been discussed previously. Anyone who is interested in more elaborate discussion of construct validity is referred to the American Psychological Association's *Standards on Educational and Psychological Tests* (1974). Synthetic validity is another type of validity which is more a combination of the more basic types. A clearer discussion of that topic can be found in Robert Guion's *Personnel Testing* (1965).

Reliability has been previously discussed as one of the four qualities of a sound selection system. I would like to spend a brief period talking about a few ways of *measuring* that reliability.

As a scientific event, if the measure of gravity on one day is fifteen pounds per inch and under exactly the same conditions two days later it is seven pounds per square inch, then gravity as a scientific phenomenon is questionable, or at least the measure of it is. The same is true for test results. A test *must be reliable* in order to be valid. If a test is not reliable, it cannot be consistently measuring anything, and certainly not what you are attempting to measure.

Test Re-test Method

To measure reliability, the scores on a test on May 20, for example, are correlated with scores which the same group earned on the same test given on May 27. Because the correlation is performed on test scores on two performances of the same test, reliability coefficients are generally much higher than validity coefficients. The former usually range in the 0.90s or 0.80s. In contrast, validity coefficients are frequently in the 0.20s and 0.30s and less frequently in the 0.40s and 0.50s. This approach to measuring reliability is called the test re-test method.

Alternate Forms Method

The test re-test method is subject to criticism because the person being tested had a chance to practice. He does better the second time around because he has practiced the test the first time. One way to satisfy this criticism is to give two forms of the same test. The test constructor builds a large sample of items in constructing the test and constructs two equivalent forms of the same test. The problem here is that it involves a great deal of work in building alternate forms.

Split-half Method

One of the most common methods of testing reliability is the split-half method. This approach splits the test into two equal parts (usually the odd numbered items constitute one-half and the even-numbered items constitute the second half). The procedure also involves scoring each half test separately and correlating scores on one-half with the second half. The obvious benefit of this approach is that it requires only one test administration and only one test form to measure internal consistency or reliability. However, the price one pays for that convenience is the inability to measure the amount of consistency occurring from one test administration to another. In addition, the reliability of so-called speed tests cannot be assessed using the split-half method. Speed tests are tests involving a stringent time period (e.g. a reading test).

The Standard Error of Measurement

A test score is a *measurement* or an approximation of a person's ability, aptitude, personal characteristics, or whatever the test is measuring. How accurate is that measurement? We do not know exactly what the true score is, but if the score is accurate, statistically speaking, repeated administrations of the test should result in scores which center around the true score. It may be a little high on one measurement and a little low on the other, but by and large these repeated measurements should result in a distribution of scores which centers around the true score and which has a standard deviation. The standard deviation of these distributions of repeated measures on the same test is called the standard error of measurement. It can be computed if one knows the correlation of the total test or the reliability of the total test. The formula for the standard error of measurement is: $SE = SD \sqrt{1 - r_t}$ where $SD =$ the standard deviation of the distribution (of the actual test scores) and r_t the reliability coefficient of the test.

In this way the standard error of measurement is used to determine the range in which the true score of an individual probably lies. If the score of an individual is 80 and the standard error of measurement is 4, we can say that his actual ability level on that test is between the values of $80 - 4$ and $80 + 4$ $(76 - 84)$. More specifically, if we were to administer the same test over and over to the same person (and control for practice which would be very difficult) two out of three times the person's score would fall between 76 and 84 and 96 percent of the time his score would fall between the values of $80 - 8$ and $80 + 8$ or 72 and 88.

Standardization

In addition to being valid and reliable, predictors which are to be quantified should be standardized as well. In other words, they should be administered under "standard conditions." What does that mean?

All predictors are no more than a sample of behavior. Sometimes that behavior is characterized by marks on a piece of paper (in a paper and pencil test). Other times they are replies in an interview (oral board) or how many push-ups one can do (physical fitness test). The need for standardization becomes apparent when we examine a test which lacks that quality. For example, suppose we give a physical fitness test and require some candidates to do as many push-ups as they can *without stopping*. Others we give a five-minute rest period. The total number of push-ups obtained per person is not accurately reflective of physical fitness because the conditions under which the test was administered were not standard. Not following established time limits or tests in distraction filled rooms are other examples of nonadherence to standardization.

An extreme case of nonstandardization is when one group is given a thirty-minute time limit with no chance to consult references and another group is given the test, told to take it home and bring it back in three weeks and finish it in any way they wish. Obviously, the latter group has a distinct advantage and no valid conclusion can be drawn from comparison of the two groups.

The final quality which refers primarily to scoring the test results involves objectivity. If a test cannot be scored independently by two different scorers with the same result, then the test lacks objectivity. A good example of this is found in academic circles where a term paper is given a C by one teacher and the same paper with a different title page and a different author's name is turned into another teacher and receives an A+. The discrepancy in scores is an indication of lack of objectivity.

The quality of objectivity has been given undue consideration in civil service examinations where almost always the test results are objective. In fact, this quality has been overemphasized in many cases at the expense of some other qualities such as validity (see O'Leary, 1976) .

Significance

The other day I received a letter from another psychologist who reported a validity coefficient between his predictor and success on the job was 0.20. If the question has not already occurred to you, let me pose it now—Is that validity coefficient good or bad? First of all, we are generally hoping that our validity coefficients would be strong or high. For example, 0.40 or 0.50 as a validity coefficient between a predictor and a criterion is very strong and quite rare.

In contrast, validity coefficients below 0.10 are undesirable as a general rule. What about the specific correlation coefficient of 0.20? Can we say more than "Oh, it's not bad and it's not good?"

The fact of the matter is, there is a specific method that can be used to evaluate the strength and importance of a specific statistic such as a correlation coefficient or a validity coefficient.

It is a very simple and direct procedure requiring that one know the strength of the correlation (e.g. 0.20) and the number of cases (n) involved in the sample in which the correlation coefficient was computed. These two data are used to enter a table and get the answer to the question, "Is this correlation coefficient high or low?"

Before going into the mechanical procedure, a word should be stated regarding the thinking behind such a procedure. Statistics is a game of numbers and there must be some way to evaluate the significance of those numbers. When one develops a statistic such as a correlation coefficient, there must be a method of determining whether the statistic arrived at was caused by chance factors or whether the correlation is so high that something other than chance is probably causing it.

In order to understand significance and the concept of statistical significance (which is different than the laymen's term of significance), a couple of day to day examples may be helpful. Assume that you get up at an early hour in the morning and at 6:30 AM you are walking to the store to get a pack of cigarettes. The first day that you do this, you pass a thirty-year-old male going in the opposite direction. The second day you pass the same male. The first day you passed him, you could feel that he had to be up for some reason and was obviously going somewhere. The second day you start to entertain a hunch that he may have a job which requires that he get up early. The third day you see him, your hunch is further substantiated, and you begin to believe that there is some systematic explanation for the fact that he is up and on the street at the same time you are. In other words, it is not just chance factors that are causing both of you to be on the street at the same time. Some systematic process (your need for cigarettes and his having to be somewhere at roughly 7:00 AM) is the factor causing the observed phenomenon.

When there is something besides chance factors affecting observed behavior, whether it be test scores or a person on the street at a certain time, statisticians refer to that as being statistically significant. Consequently, nonsignificant and chance are essentially synonymous.

Here is another example. You are driving down the street and you notice a late model Chrysler ™ behind you. As you make a right turn, the Chrysler makes a right turn also. At that point, there is a slight suggestion that the car may be following you, but because you turned off a busy street onto another busy street that probability is not very significant. Now you make a left turn onto a less busy street and the Chrysler does the same. This still could be just a chance occurrence. The Chrysler could be going in your same general direction by chance but the probability that he is following your specific automobile is increased. After a series of three or four more turns, the probability is very high that the car is following yours.

Look at that last sentence. When one says that the probability is very high, he is essentially saying that there is some significant degree of correlation between your turns and the Chrysler's turns to suggest that it is more than just chance. We are still not 100 percent sure that the car is following you. Although it is improbable (the probability is low) that the Chrysler is going to the exact same street and the driver is visiting someone else on the same street or even the same person at the same time, it is possible. We might say that the chances out of 100 of that occurring are very small, say 1 out of 100, but it is possible.

Now we have two possible explanation categories: one, simply by chance occurrence that car has gone to the same location (the probability of this happening is say 1 out of 100) ; two, the car was following you. There may be a third or a fourth explanation, but the example is used simply to point out the difference between chance occurrence and a significant phenomenon. It is rare in statistics or in testing that one can say with 100 percent certainty that such and such exists. Instead, we can make stronger or weaker probability statements (statements of significance) .

One final example, in the testing field there has been a lot of talk about cultural fairness of tests and discrimination against minorities. This issue will be treated in depth later on, but take an example of a situation where the sergeant's promotional test has been administered to 200 applicants. Of the 200, let us assume 150 are white males and 50 are black males. Being good test analysts, we compute the mean and standard deviation for each of the two distributions. In so doing, we find that the average score on the test for the white sample is eighty-five and for the black sample is eighty. Whenever you take two samples, you will rarely obtain an identical average for both samples. Therefore, the question becomes "Is the five-point difference between the two sample averages significant or is it just a matter of chance?" There is a statistical test to answer that question and it is called a "T" test (developed by "Student"). The formula for "Student's" T is as follows:

$$T = \frac{\overline{X}_1 - \overline{X}_2}{SD_1 - SD_2}$$

The resulting number or T value is used along with the number of people in each sample to enter a table of significance. So one goes to the T distribution table with the T value and number of people in the sample. One comes away from the table with a value indicating the chances out of 100 that this difference would occur *if chance alone was operative.*

If the number brought away from the table is 0.37, this means that in 37 cases out of 100 the obtained statistic, in this case the T value, could be achieved by chance alone. Similarly, if the obtained significance level or probability statement coming away from the table was 0.73, the interpretation would be that in 73 cases out of 100 this difference could be achieved by chance alone.

It should become apparent to the reader that the lower the probability value (P), the more significant the statistic that it is being used to evaluate. In other words, if the probability statement coming away from the table is 0.01, then this is interpreted as meaning the chance of the statistic, or in this case the differences in the two averages, being caused by chance factors only is 1 out of 100, very small. *Therefore, the probability that something other than chance is operating is very high (i.e. 99 out of 100).*

This same procedure can be used to evaluate other statistics such as correlation coefficients to determine how significant they are. Scientific convention has established a probability value of 0.05 and another one of 0.01 as being bench marks in terms of acceptable levels of probability. If statistics reach this probability level, the scientific community tends to sit up and take notice in many cases. This is assuming that the research methodology is done correctly. The Equal Employment Opportunity Commission, which will be discussed later, has adopted 0.05 level of probability in its guideline as determining the acceptability of certain validity coefficients.

Another way of stating this is that if a validity coefficient is so high that it is obtainable by chance alone only 5 times in 100, it is acceptable by the EEOC. (This may be occasionally stated as 1 out of 20, which is the equivalent of 5 out of 100.) It should be noted here that there is a significance table in Appendix D.

Chapter 4

PERFORMANCE MEASURES

Predicting Job Performance

I F A DEPARTMENT's objective in developing a selection system is to predict job performance, then it is important for the department to be able to measure and identify both successful and unsuccessful performance in a specific position. Measuring job performance can be an elusive objective. However, you should be aware that there are a number of basic ideas to remember which help guide the practitioner through some troubled waters.

The development of a sound performance measure or criterion starts at the same place where one would begin to develop a sound predictor system—namely, at the job analysis.

The job elements would be examined and a logical approach would be used to try and develop performance measures that would reflect success in the major job elements. In the examples that we gave before, one might use the task statements as one point to examine tasks performed and then come to some decision about the method of measuring this job performance as reflected in each individual task.

Multidimensional Measures

Anyone who has done a job analysis on a position even though it may be very routine on the outside recognizes that the successful job performance is not a single entity or factor. In point of fact, every job is broken down into a number of job components each of which may be quite independent from another. The police officer whose knowledge of the law and willingness to enforce it are very high, could be judged as an excellent performer but such an evaluation may ignore other facets of the job such as the fact that he is rarely on the job at the assigned time or that he has difficulty in interacting with persons who are not law violators.

34

Performance Measures and Validating Selection Systems

Tying this topic of job performance measures (frequently called criteria in the literature) to the purpose of this book, the validity of a selection system is closely tied to demonstrating effectiveness of the selection system by showing it is related to some criterion. This is true with any type of validity model that is being used. That was previously discussed in Chapter 4 but it is particularly important in generating criterion-related validity. In fact, a department could actually have a sound selection system but if they do not develop sound criterion, an attempt to demonstrate criterion-related validity may be a failure causing them to throw out a selection system which, in reality, is valid.

Categories of Criteria

Having recognized that the job analysis is the start of looking for indicators of successful performance, we now are faced with the practical consideration of how to measure these performance qualities. A general rule in this whole area is that an objective measure of job performance is superior from a measurement standpoint to a subjective measure. Examples of objective measures would be such things as numbers of days absent or numbers of arrests made within a given period of time, as opposed to such subjective measures as performance ratings by a superior, peer ratings, or other ratings that require some judgmental act.

Subjective Versus Objective Criteria

Therefore, we can order the whole area of performance measures or criteria by saying that there are two broad categories—objective and subjective. The objective measures are preferable from a measuring standpoint; that is, they are more exact and defensible from a psychometric point of view, but they frequently suffer from other problems, particularly job relatedness. For example, some have focused on numbers of arrests as a criterion. The assumption has been that the officer who makes more arrests is performing his duty to a greater degree than the officer who makes fewer arrests. In some situations, it may be an appropriate assumption, but in others it is very questionable. A police officer may be assigned to an area of the city which is a high crime area where he only makes half the arrests he actually should. His arrests may exceed the number made by another police officer who is doing an excellent job in a low crime area.

The number of citizen complaints being made about a particular police officer is another objective criterion which suffers from a similar problem. Typically, the officer receiving fewer citizens' complaints is perceived as doing a better job than the officer who receives a substantial number. This logic may hold true in certain situations; however, many middle-management police personnel believe that a police officer who has few or no citizen complaints in his file is probably playing it safe at the expense of his job. I am not saying that these criteria should never be used, however, there are some assumptions which should be questioned before putting such objective measures into place as indicators of successful job performance.

If the department, after having reviewed the assumptions, can honestly say that "numbers of arrests," "numbers of citizens' complaints," and related objective measures are true reflections of successful police performance in their department, then they could implement them as bonafide, job-related criteria for that position. In fact, the psychometric soundness of these criteria would mean that they had a valuable kind of performance measure.

There are other objective measures which are less subject to the problem of faulty assumptions. These criteria are such things as "days absent" or "times tardy" which are both objective and typically agreed upon by most people as job-related measures of on-job performance.

If the reader can identify some predictor which will identify people who will consistently be late or absent from work before they hire them, then such a predictor can be used as a valid component of the final selection system.

In an unpublished study of a skilled trade union, I identified "number of days absent in high school" as a predictor for attendance on the job as a journeyman. In other words, it was statistically demonstrated what some people may conclude by common sense—namely, the candidates whose high school record showed a substantial number of absences generally had higher absenteeism records as journeymen.

There are a number of other objective criteria but one other worth mentioning is that of voluntary turnover, In certain occupations, selectors like to have a predictor of the likelihood that a person would quit the job within a relatively brief period of time after having accepted it. This is another component of success for job performance—namely, job tenure.

The reader who is interested in predictors that have effectively measured and predicted job tenure is referred to studies in bio-data by Owens and Buel.

Subjective Performance Measures

If highly job-related aspects of job performance are not measurable by objective measures (and this is almost always the case), then there are only a few options open. One of these is the use of subjective or judgmental performance measures. The most common example of this is a supervisor rating of a particular police officer's performance. An example of such a rating form is included here to serve as an example (see Figure 2).

Each quality or dimension to be measured on the form should be tied directly to some major job element of the position which has been previously derived from the job analysis. This is a further example of the importance of a good job analysis.

Scaling

Once you have some sort of a rating form and have decided which qualities you are going to rate, you must then choose a scale to record these ratings. There are many varieties but the most common scales are five– and seven-point scales with occasional three-point or ten-point scales.

A very widely used scale is the Likert scale which involves five points ranging from a one which is very low to a five which is very high. The scale used depends on the purpose and how comfortable one feels with it. There is a trade off in using different scales. Using a very basic scale (e.g. 1—below average, 2—average, 3—

above average) allows the discriminations to be made by the raters to be very broad and less difficult than those required by a seven– or nine-point scale. However, the latter provide for more variation than a three-point scale. Use of a three-point scale also leads to complaints by raters that a ratee is somewhere between average and outstanding, and the scale does not allow for such a rating. The following is an example of a nine-point rating scale developed with the help of detectives and detective supervisors who contributed the critical incidents listed under each quality.

Candidate's Name: _____

Rater's Name: _____

Date: _____

Facilitator's Name: _____

Performance Rating of a
Rochester Police Officer
on Key Job-Related Skills and
Abilities Important For The
Position of Investigator

CONFIDENTIAL

Figure 2.

DECISIVENESS—Readiness to make decisions or to render judgments.

CIRCLE
ONE
RATING:

---9---

EXAMPLES OF GOOD DECISIVENESS

Police officers seeking a suspect in a hospital encountered a doctor who refused to release the suspect to their custody. After determining that there was no medical reason for the doctor to keep the suspect in the hospital, the officers took the suspect forcefully from the hospital. Their high degree of decisiveness paid off when it was later determined that they were right in taking the man over the objections from the doctor.

---8---

---7---

An officer responded to a reported dispute involving two tavern patrons, Jones and Smith, each claiming ownership of a $10 bill which was on the bar. The officer listened to each of them and gave the money to Jones. (Subsequently, it was learned that the $10 actually belonged to Smith. The officer's decision was the wrong one, but it was made readily.)

---6---

---5---

AVERAGE PERFORMANCE

---4---

EXAMPLES OF POOR DECISIVENESS

An officer responded to a report of a theft from a small jewelry store. The proprietor claimed that a teenage youth still on the premises had taken a wristwatch which he put in his sock. The proprietor demanded that the youth be arrested and searched. The teenager threatened to sue the officer if the officer touched him. The officer went to radio a request for his sergeant to come to the scene to advise the officer. When he re-entered the shop, the teenager and the wristwatch were gone.

---3---

---2---

A police officer investigating a motor vehicle accident believed that one of the drivers involved was intoxicated. Unsure if chemical evidence would support an arrest for DWI, the officer asked the driver if he would submit to a breathalyzer test. The driver agreed without being arrested. The breathalyzer results showed that the driver was intoxicated and the officer then arrested him. The case was dismissed because of the officer's reluctance to make a decision. The law requires that the test must be administered within two hours AFTER arrest.

---1---

Figure 2 Continued.

JUDGMENT——Ability to reach logical conclusions based on the evidence at hand.

CIRCLE
ONE
RATING:

---9---

EXAMPLES OF SOUND JUDGMENT

An officer who was first to respond to a reported break-in in progress at a warehouse noted that the rear of the building could not be readily reached from the street upon which it was located. Concluding that apprehension of suspects would be very difficult if they fled by way of the rear of the building, he requested additional cars to go to an adjacent street from which officers could easily reach the rear of the warehouse. He delayed approaching the front of the building until officers were deployed at the rear.

---8---

---7---

A police officer observed three Spanish men walking through a primarily black neighborhood; one of the men fit the description of a man involved in several armed robberies in the neighborhood. Before approaching the men, he quietly called for another police car. When he asked the suspect to get into the police car, all three men objected; but they withdrew their objections when the other cars arrived.

---6---

---5---

AVERAGE PERFORMANCE

---4---

EXAMPLES OF POOR JUDGMENT

A police car answered a call that a sniper was shooting at passers-by. The officers left their car headlights on and stood in front of them, talking to each other. The sniper could easily have shot the officers.

---3---

---2---

A policeman responded to a bank alarm at 9:15 AM. Since the bank only opened at 9:00 AM. he concluded that it was a false alarm. When he entered the bank alone with his service revolver holstered, he was confronted by a robber who locked him in the vault.

---1---

Figure 2 Continued.

PLANNING AND ORGANIZATION——Effectiveness in planning and organizing own activities and those of a group.

CIRCLE
ONE
RATING:

---9---

---8---

EXAMPLES OF GOOD PLANNING AND ORGANIZATION

In approaching a house in which a suspect was reportedly identified, the officers surrounded the house so that the criminal had no possible way to escape.

---7---

An officer was notified that one of his cases was scheduled for trial, but believing it might be adjourned, he contacted his witnesses two days before the scheduled trial date. He made arrangements to telephone them on the morning of the scheduled trial date to advise them if they would be required to appear. The case was adjourned, the witnesses were grateful for the officer's thoughtfulness and, when the case finally was tried, all witnesses appeared without complaining. The suspect was convicted.

---6---

---5---

AVERAGE PERFORMANCE

---4---

EXAMPLES OF POOR PLANNING AND ORGANIZATION

An officer, about to be relieved from duty was responding to a still alarm of fire. He was first on the scene and parked his police vehicle directly in front of the fire location. Fire equipment arriving a few minutes later blocked the street and the officer's vehicle. When an officer from a succeeding platoon arrived to relieve him, the officer who first responded was unable to leave the scene.

---3---

---2---

Before going downtown to fill his car with gasoline, an officer failed to call the dispatcher to find out whether the garage was open. When he arrived, he found the garage closed and was forced to make another trip later in his tour of duty.

---1---

Figure 2 Continued.

PROBLEM ANALYSIS—Effectiveness in seeking out pertinent data and in determining the source of the problem.

CIRCLE
ONE
RATING:

---9---

---8---

---7---

---6---

---5---

---4---

---3---

---2---

---1---

EXAMPLES OF GOOD PROBLEM ANALYSIS

EXAMPLES OF POOR PROBLEM ANALYSIS

A gas station attendant claimed that he had been pushed down and robbed of the station receipts. The policeman noticed that there was no dirt or marks on the attendant's shirt. He further questioned the attendant who admitted he had fabricated the story, and produced the missing funds from where they had been hidden in his shoe.

Over a period of several months one or two rooms in a local hotel were burglarized each week. The investigator assigned to the most recent burglary determined that entry had been gained in each case by use of a duplicate or master key. He checked the hotel register and found one of three different names listed as occupants of the ransacked rooms about one week before each burglary. Noting one of the three names on the register for room 212 three days earlier, he arranged a stake-out of the room. The following night the suspect entered the room and was apprehended. All the burglaries were cleared when the suspect admitted he had used aliases when checking in and had duplicated the keys to the rooms he occupied.

AVERAGE PERFORMANCE

A police officer was interrogating a suspect when the officer's partner walked in and said "We know you did it because we have your fingerprints." The first officer, however, had already determined that the suspect was wearing gloves, and this completely destroyed the credibility of the officers.

A police officer investigated a report of a hit and run accident involving right-side damage to a vehicle while it was allegedly parked at the curb in front of the owner's home. He failed to deduce that the damage could not have occurred as reported unless the striking vehicle had been driven between the curb and the sidewalk leaving tire tracks in the lawn. Several days later, the Hit and Run Squad arrested the reporting owner for leaving the scene of an accident which resulted in the damage observed by the officer. Considerable time and effort would have been saved if the officer had gathered and properly analyzed the available facts.

Figure 2 Continued.

IMPACT—Ability to create a good first impression, to command attention and respect, to show an air of confidence, and to achieve personal recognition.

CIRCLE
ONE
RATING:

---9---

EXAMPLES OF GOOD IMPACT

An officer effectively interrogates suspect, confronting him with inconsistencies and falsehoods in his story, introducing evidence and facts showing suspect's relation to the crime, to shock or surprise him with incriminating statements.

---8---

In an incident involving a child being hit by a car driven by an old lady, the officer arrived on the scene, calmly spoke with the parents of the child, and made members of the crowd realize that it was an accident, and not deliberate. The impact of the officer was particularly obvious because the racial difference between the person driving the car and the crowd made the situation especially touchy.

---7---

---6---

---5---   AVERAGE PERFORMANCE

---4---

---3---

EXAMPLES OF POOR IMPACT

A police officer, in approaching a traffic violator, says, "Where the hell are you going, to a race?" This immediately generates a hostile atmosphere, since the officer has no idea of why the person was speeding.

---2---

A mother concerned about her son's unkempt appearance chastises the boy. A noisy argument ensues and the police are summoned. The officer responding is not wearing his uniform cap, needs a shave and haircut, and his uniform is not clean and neatly pressed. He counsels the youngster upon the importance of personal grooming. When the officer leaves, the son cites him as an example supporting his slovenly life-style — the mother files a personal complaint against the policeman.

---1---

Figure 2 Continued.

INITIATIVE——Actively influencing events rather than passive-ly accepting; self-starting.

CIRCLE
ONE
RATING:

---9---   A police officer was on sick leave as a result of a broken leg incurred in the line of duty. His physician had not authorized his return to work. The officer contacted the police physician requesting that he be permitted to return to some light duty assignment. The police physician identified a light duty assignment and the officer's services were made available to the department.

---8---

---7---   A police officer on patrol observes a vehicle parked during the nighttime hours in a location where vehicles are not usually parked. He checks several buildings in the area and finds nothing out of order. He records the license plate number of the vehicle, obtains a 1028, and submits a field interview form. The following day a burglary is discovered on an adjacent street. Investigators follow up on the information provided by the officer and find that the vehicle was involved in the burglary and the burglars are arrested.

---6---

---5---   AVERAGE PERFORMANCE

---4---   A police officer on an assignment resolves the problem and is completing the paperwork in his vehicle when he hears another unit assigned to a call for service close by. The officer fails to advise the dispatcher that he can take the assignment with the result that another unit must cover in the offending officer's territory.

---3---

---2---   An officer operating a patrol vehicle notices that the temperature gauge indicates an unusually high temperature in the motor. He fails to take the vehicle to the garage but merely notes the condition on his activity report. The officer assigned to that vehicle on the succeeding platoon discovers that the engine has been damaged as a result of the excessive temperature.

---1---

EXAMPLES OF GOOD INITIATIVE

EXAMPLES OF POOR INITIATIVE

Figure 2 Continued.

OTHER DIMENSIONS

Rater's definition:

---9---

Rater's example —— good

---8---

---7---

---6---

---5---   AVERAGE PERFORMANCE

---4---

Rater's example —— poor

---3---

---2---

---1---

NOTE: ARE THESE EXAMPLES MORE PROPERLY DE-
SCRIPTIVE OF ONE OF THE DIMENSIONS AL-
READY DISCUSSED?

FACILITATOR'S COMMENTS

(NOTE: A facilitator was a member of a small group of personnel trained in the procedure of gathering behaviorally anchored
ratings from supervisors and peers.)

Figure 2 Continued.

RATING ANCHORS

---9---	Consistently displays positive indicators of this quality, rarely displaying negative indicators.
---8---	
---7---	Overall, the officer's performance in this area reflects a far greater degree of positive indicators than negative indicators.
---6---	
---5---	Average performance -- behavior in this area, like that of many other officers, reflects some positive and some negative indicators.
---4---	
---3---	Overall, the officer's performance in this area reflects a far greater degree of negative indicators than positive indicators.
---2---	
---1---	Consistently displays negative indicators of this quality, rarely displaying positive indicators.

Remember ——avoid

(1) Leniency error

(2) Halo error

(3) Central tendency error

Figure 2 Continued.

The reason for the popularity of a five– or seven-point scale is that a three-point scale allows for only average, outstanding, and very low, but a high number scale creates a difficulty in distinguishing between such points as a five or a six.

Common Errors Associated With Rating Scales

In developing a rating scale that is job related and clearly reflects performance on the job, one should be aware of some very common errors involved in rating scales. This list does not attempt to be exhaustive but lists only the major types of error.

CENTRAL TENDENCY ERROR: Filling out rating forms is not the most enjoyable task in the world. This is particularly true for a busy first-line or mid-management person in a police department.

They have major responsibilities and frequently are eager to get on with "doing what they are paid for." It is not unexpected, therefore, for a rater to approach a rating scale with an attitude of getting the thing done as quickly as possible.

One way to remain inconspicuous and do the job quickly is to "hug the middle" of the rating scale. If you rate your subordinates as average with one or two qualities a little above average, then most people are satisfied. This tendency to rate people average even when their performance is anything but average is known as central tendency error.

Because many supervisors do not want to either (1) alienate their subordinates by giving them below average ratings, or (2) have to justify to their superiors why they have subordinates who are below average in some areas of their work, the vast majority of performance ratings recorded by supervisors are within the upper half of the scale (i.e. either three, four, or five, on a five-point scale or four, five, six, or seven on a seven-point scale). This type of error, which I have labeled the PYI error (Protect Your Interests) not only exaggerates the central tendency error but also creates another problem.

If you will recall, I mentioned that it was very important to have differences in scores on the predictors one uses for predicting job success. The same thing is true for the criterion or performance measures gathered. If only half of the performance rating scale is used, namely the upper half, then the range of scores being earned is dramatically reduced and a restriction of range problem is created.

There are a number of ways to reduce the effects of the central tendency error although none of them can be completely eliminated. One of the first suggestions is to meet with the raters before they complete their rating form, stress the problem, and emphasize that they should use high ratings or low ratings when appropriate. Many times raters are really unconscious of the fact that they are committing these errors and will frequently respond to such pretraining. Such training is very helpful in setting the proper climate for the ratings and can contribute substantially to accurate performance ratings.

Another way to deal with this problem of central tendency is to use a seven-point scale and move the average point down to a two or three rather than a four. This allows people to use more of the scale for rating their people without pushing them to rate below average.

One other solution is to define each of the points of the scale with some behavioral examples. This can be done by first getting a group of incumbents together and asking them to generate critical incidents of behavior which could be labeled as clearly good performance or clearly poor performance (Flanagan, 1953).

In many cases, a person will rate a candidate as average simply because they have a very foggy impression of what average means. In some cases, when specific examples of job-related behavior can be listed, the rater is more likely to give a rating of above or below the midpoint when appropriate. An example of such a critical incident approach was used at the Rochester (New York) Police Department where I developed anchor points or "definitions by example" for the scales after conducting interviews with groups of incumbent investigators within the department (see Figure 2).

HALO ERROR: If punctuality is the quality being rated and a given officer is extremely punctual, halo error would occur if that officer would get high ratings on other qualities simply because his punctuality was thought important by the rater. In other words, there is a tendency to see many of these qualities running together and consequently have a rating on one of them influence a rating of the other. "He's a good old boy" is the kind of attitude which can easily lead to halo error.

One way to deal with halo error is to make the rater consciously aware that he should view each quality as independent and distinct.

A second way is to request that the rater rate all of the subordinates on Scale 1 before going to Scale 2 and so on.

JOB EXTRANEOUS ERROR: A final type of rating error occurs when the rating is based on feelings or behavior extraneous to the dimension or quality being rated. Such an error is exemplified by an officer receiving a poor rating on a job-related component such as "effectiveness in completing assigned tasks" because the rater resents the fact that the officer does not call him "sir" when he addresses him. The reader can probably think of other examples of job extraneous error.

Solutions to this error again include making the rater aware of it and using job specific anchor points to reduce the effects of job extraneous error. However, the major tool in combating this type of error is multiple ratings of a given officer, when possible. If there are two people who supervise the officer's work, then obtaining two *independent* measures will reduce the effects of job extraneous error occurring in one of the ratings.

Emphasis is put on the fact that these ratings should be independent. The common practice of asking a sergeant and then his lieutenant to rate a police officer does not produce independent results if, as is often the case, the lieutenant is given the sergeant's rating to agree or disagree with. For two reasons this is not an adequate solution: (1) the lieutenant is privy to the sergeant's rating and thereby does not give an independent rating in all cases and (2) the lieutenant is usually one step removed from actual performance by the police officer and will frequently rely on the sergeant's judgment. This method works in those situations where both raters are almost equally familiar with the officer's performance on the job.

When this is not possible, another solution is to obtain anonymous ratings from officers who are in the same squad as the participant.

Such peer ratings can be used in conjunction with a single supervisor rating and ultimately generate a more accurate picture of the officer's actual job performance. This approach was taken in the selection system used for investigator in the Rochester Police Department and appeared to work fairly well.

One disadvantage of all rating systems is that the people rated may come out very close. This causes the possibility of ties in ratings. However, this can be avoided by using a ranking system.

Ranking Systems

A ranking system forces the supervisor to assign different ranks to all of his people. From a measurement standpoint this is advantageous since it does not allow for ties. However, as the reader can imagine, many supervisors resist ranking their people from the best performer to the lowest performer.

The major complaints about rankings by those people who are required to do them is not with the extreme rank. A supervisor will usually report that it is not difficult to rank his best performer or his number two, three, four, or even five person in terms of a given quality, neither does he have difficulty in identifying his poorest performer or second poorest performer, etc. The problem arises in the middle of the ranks. For example, if fifteen or twenty officers are to be ranked, the distinction between numbers nine and ten is very difficult to make sometimes rather arbitrary.

When this problem does occur, one possible solution is to require that the ranker identify the top third of his subordinates and the bottom third. Since the remainder fall in the middle third, the ranker has successfully generated three distinct groups which can be useful as a performance measure. This solution has the additional and substantial advantage of being much easier for the rankers.

Another solution is a variation known as the "paired comparison" technique. Obviously it is easier to judge which of two workers is superior than to rank the numbers of a large group.

To administer this technique of "paired comparison," the ranker is given a series of cards containing two names per card. The rater then checks the name of the individual he considers the better of the two on each card. The final ranking of the workers is determined by the number of times each was judged better than the others.

One of the major drawbacks of the method is that the amount of work that must be performed is greatly increased, particularly as the number of people being rated increases. The number of judgments that have to be made for a group of ten officers would be $\frac{N(N-1)}{2}$. If there were four employees, this means 6 comparisons; for ten employees, there are 45 comparisons; and if there are fifty people in the group, the rater must make 1,225 separate comparisons.

The other drawback to this approach is that it applies only to people who are going to make an overall global ranking of their people. For this reason it is not very frequently used.

Another method that has helped in reducing many rater errors is to train a cadre of handpicked people (facilitators) to complete the rating forms while interviewing supervisors and asking key questions and giving examples of good and poor performance. In the police department of Rochester, New York, lieutenants were selected as the facilitators. However it should be emphasized that such a procedure must heavily stress both handpicking the raters and a thorough training program.

One other approach to measuring job performance is a job simulation exercise. One might set up a series of job simulations in which the police officer would take what he feels appropriate action would be. This performance would be observed by a number of raters. This job simulation approach to performance measures has numerous advantages including standardized exercises, multiple raters, and ratings based on very recent behavioral observations. The major disadvantage is that job simulation exercises would have to be developed and time scheduled to go through these measures. In addition, there would have to be a close tie between the simulations and actual job performance.

In summing up this area of performance ratings, I should emphasize that there are some basic steps which can be taken to minimize errors. The first is to develop clear and concise definitions of the qualities to be used as a reflection of effective job performance. These should be tied directly into each stage of an accurate job analysis.

The second is to recognize that there is no one perfect measuring device for generating accurate job performance measures. In fact, the best approximation is probably a multidimensional one since all jobs are multidimensional.

Finally, whether an organization elects to use ranking systems, behaviorally-anchored scales, or a five-point scale, it is critical to begin with a training session for the raters (this term includes rankers). The training session should include an indication of the standard types of errors encountered in ratings, a clear definition of each of the components to be rated, and the importance of the exercise since the job performance measures are very important to the organization.

Chapter 5

A SAMPLE SELECTION SYSTEM

THE OBJECTIVE of this book, as was previously stated, is to provide each department with a step by step procedure which they can follow in (1) determining whether their selection system is valid and (2) assisting them in identifying what types of predictors to use for the different positions. Up to this point, we have discussed some fundamental techniques in job analysis, quantification, and performance appraisal. Now we will look at an actual selection system as one model for the reader to consider.

You should be cautioned about putting too much emphasis on specific predictors used at any one point in the selection system. I believe that the system described here is a good one but that any single component could be questioned. In sum, you are urged to consider the selection system as a totality. If it works for your department then you are encouraged to use it. If it does not work merely because of a special problem relating to one specific component, then modify that component but retain the system.

Consistent with the systems approach initiated early in the book, the first step in developing a selection system would be to conduct a thorough job analysis which would yield the knowledges, skills, abilities, and personal characteristics (KSAPCs) required for the position. One of the most difficult positions for which to develop a selection system is that of entry level police officer. Because promotional selection systems will be considered later in the book, this sample selection system will use the generic position of entry level police officer as its target position.

Once the KSAPCs have been identified, a test plan should be developed. Such a test plan involves a listing of the KSAPCs down the left-hand column of a chart and an indication of which predictor component (e.g. paper and pencil test, interview, medical examination) will measure that particular KSAPC. In some cases, the particular KSAPC may be unmeasurable. In such instances, it should be so indicated. A sample test plan is found in Appendix G.

In the figure you will notice that the predictor components of the selection system are listed across the top of the figure while the KSAPCs are listed down the left-hand column. The reader may be able to think of more predictor components. The figure is not offered as an exhaustive one. However, a few things should be pointed out. First of all, the reader will notice that certain KSAPCs are measured by more than one component. For example, the ability to effectively interact with fellow officers (KSAPC 6) is measured in the oral board, in the psychiatric interview, and in the working test period.

There is a general principle that one should measure a KSAPC wherever one can possibly do so. Do not believe that once you have measured a KSAPC in one component you are finished looking at it. Remember, the entire selection system is a probability statement regarding the *"probable success"* of the candidate. One's selection batting average can be increased and thereby the probability of success by measuring KSAPCs whenever and however possible.

I have attempted to list the components in the order in which they would appear in the selection procedure. So the application review occurs prior to the written test which in turn occurs prior to the medical or psychiatric examination. A physical condition or a physical performance test could be implemented and if it were, it should come after the medical exam. It should be located there for two reasons: (1) Before putting a candidate through a vigorous performance test, his general medical condition should be established as strong enough to withstand such a test. (2) A physical condition test is usually quite expensive to set up. For further discussion of physical fitness tests within the police field, one is referred to an article by Forbes McCann in a volume on testing entitled *Recruitment and Selection in the Public Service* by J. J. Donovan (1967).

Effective Use of a Selection System

Typically, one tries to put the least expensive selection components at the front of the system so that the department's use of

resources is minimized until a candidate becomes a serious con-
tender for the position. It is not only wasteful in terms of the
department's time but very inconsiderate to the candidate to
allow him to progress along in the system when an early component clearly disqualifies him. Selection programs which do not
heed this consideration cause serious discontent among candidates
and frustration on the part of selection and recruitment personnel. This is another reason for the department to have clear
guidelines and specifications as to what the selection components
will involve and how they are justified.

There is always a tendency for selection personnel to overlook
a particular qualification or stretch a point to enable a candidate
to pass through a particular selection component. While I can
see the justification for this in some unusual instances, one should
recognize that such "goodheartedness" may have two negative
effects. It can (1) allow people into the position whose probability of success is relatively small and (2) involve the substantial
use of a disqualified candidate's time including testing, completion of forms, and medical examination when it was obvious
that he was not qualified at the beginning. So in a sense, this is
playing games with the candidate rather than being open with
him.

The selection plan should be based on a thorough job analysis
and logically tied to the KSAPCs so identified. Once those have
been established and reasonable cutoffs outlined, the selection
components should function properly. This requires that users
be trained in methods and reasons why. All too often a sound
selection system is destroyed by an inept implementation of it.

One final point before leaving the figure is the use of the working test period as a selection component. Most departments have
a probation period which involves the police training program
and the probation period on patrol. However, it has been
relegated to a rather minor role in most departments because it
has essentially become a rubber stamp. When one gets into the
program and goes through the cadet training program, usually
he is moved into permanent police officer status.

Many department officials are seeking a test approved by this
or that agency, which is culturally fair, and which can be used in

selection. In this mad rush for "the" test, many employers and police departments have overlooked a very good selection component right in their own backyard—the working test period. Since it is one of the last selection components and it occurs only after a substantial investment of time and money in the candidate, it should not reject many people. However, since it is a close approximation of the job itself, it is a powerful tool for measuring qualifications which are virtually unmeasurable by other predictors. One gets a much better measure of how effectively a candidate can understand and follow directions from his supervisor in the working test period than he does in a thirty or forty-five minute oral board. Therefore it should be used as an important predictor component.

Two elements have been lacking in the past to render the working test period as an effective predictor of job performance: (1) some formal method of evaluating the candidate's performance which is specific and job related, (2) a willingness on the part of supervisors familiar with the candidate's working test performance to rate the person as he really performs.

The first problem is rather easily solved by using some previously discussed procedures in developing a job-related performance appraisal form. It would be completed halfway through the working test period with feedback to the candidate on how he is doing. This will give him an opportunity to make improvements in his performance and will give management an opportunity to use his past feedback behavior as an additional input for their final decision at the end of the probation period. Some of the ideas and concepts in the chapter on performance appraisal could be implemented here in developing such an appraisal form. Discussions with academy instructors and probation supervisors would be a good source of information regarding kinds of behavior to be used in rating key KSAPCs for the job.

The second problem could be addressed by a training program for probation supervisors in the completion of these performance appraisal forms. The program should stress the importance of filling out the rating forms accurately. If the supervisor understands that his failure to do so might result in an unqualified person entering his department, then it is much more likely that the working test period will reach its full potential as a final selection component.

Developing a selection system for entry level patrol officers is difficult for many reasons but there are two primary ones.

(1) The "press of bodies" problem caused by the simple fact that there are a large number of applicants for a limited number of jobs. While a large selection ratio such as 400 applicants to 10 jobs makes it an employer's market, it also requires the employer to have a selection system that is not only job related and valid but easily administered. It makes little sense to develop a selection system which is valid and job related but takes four to five days for each candidate.

(2) The "testing for potential" problem caused by the fact that there are relatively few specific knowledges which have been demonstrated predictive of success in an entry level police officer position. Most of the information that a police officer will need on the job and specific knowledges that could comprise such a test would be taught to him at the police academy. Therefore it is necessary to evaluate a candidate's "potential" to learn this specific knowledge, and that is very difficult.

For example, one police department had an entry level selection system for the position of patrol officer. The one component of the system was a situation in which a police officer played the role of a youth who had just purchased a malt at a local drive-in restaurant and was sitting in his car while the lone female worker in the drive-in was closing up. She was frightened by the situation and called the police to complain that there was a suspicious looking character in the parking lot. The candidate was to play the role of the responding officer. The problem of using the candidate's behavior in this situation as a predictor of future performance is that much of the knowledge that he needed, such as legal restrictions and techniques in approaching such a person, would be taught to him in the academy.

What does one do in a testing situation like this? Certainly there have been problems in administering general intelligence tests because it has been difficult to demonstrate a relationship between performance on these tests and actual job performance. Furthermore, many of these tests of general intellectual ability have a substantial adverse impact or discriminatory effect on the selection of minorities.   The net effect is that using such a selection component at this level is the development of a non–job-related filter which filters out more members of a protected class (protected under the 1964 Civil Rights Act Title VII) and renders the department vulnerable to a discrimination charge in hiring.

What does one do? An undesirable solution in the author's mind is to fill positions based on chronological order of filing an application. Few departments have done this and when they do, it is usually a reflection of the frustration they have encountered in using any type of selection component.

A better alternative is to follow a sound job analysis with some kind of selection system beginning with tests measuring such job-related skills as reading ability and the ability to follow simple oral directions. Both of these tests can be administered in groups. In addition, both skills are important in the performance of the cadet's job both on the street and in the academy. There is a simple method for determining the reading material which has to be read both in the academy and on the street. It is certainly reasonable to require a minimum level of reading skills if that skill is going to be required in the academy setting and in the performance of the job duties. The United States Supreme Court ruled in *Davis v. Washington* that performance in the academy was a legitimate criterion against which components of a predictor system could be related.

Paper and pencil tests which currently show some promise include those developed by the selection consulting center of the California State Personnel Board and those developed by Marvin Dunnette in Minnesota. His entry level tests are objective multiple-choice tests made up of biographical information questions and other questions typically found on a job-related personality test. Unlike the traditional personality tests, Dunnette's tests are supported by hard data showing that candidates who score high on his test tend to perform better in the position of patrol officer. (Dunnette, Motowidlo, 1976).

One of the other problems associated with hiring entry level police officers arises when one tries to base a hire decision on past performance. The problem is that many of them have not had substantial job experience and some are coming to the selection process out of the military or after a year or two of college. However, we can use any type of past performance to predict job success in the academy or in the position of patrol officer, if it is valid —that is, if it predicts success on the job.

There is an old maxim that the best predictor of future performance is past performance. While this is true in many cases, the selection specialist should remember that the inclusion of components measuring past performance in a selection system will require that they be validated in some statistical fashion in most cases. In one study for a skill trade union, I needed to predict success of young high school or college students in a training program (in this case, it was the apprenticeship program). As was previously mentioned in Chapter 4, one of the interesting predictors which was validated was that of high school attendance. The study demonstrated that apprentices and journeymen who had a poor attendance record in high school also had poor attendance on the job. It is this type of data which can be used, if validated, in helping to identify the candidates who have the highest probability of succeeding on the job.

Another form of measuring a person's background is using a technique known as the *bio-data form*. The bio-data approach involves the administration of a substantial number of objective questions about the person's background references, etc., all in a multiple-choice format. It is usually administered in group form and has been successfully developed so that it can predict such things as the probability of a candidate remaining as a police officer once, he is hired (voluntary turnover). In those situations where voluntary turnover is a problem, the bio-data form is a very promising selection component. In some cases, the bio-data form has been used in predicting other aspects of successful performance as a police officer as well.

The broad steps in installing such a bio-data form are as follows:

1. Develop a preliminary questionnaire. A series of background information items are generated from such lists as

those developed by the Richardson Foundation (1966). In many cases, in excess of 150 items should be listed.

2. Identify a criterion, such as tenure, among the incumbents in the police officer ranks.
3. Administer the questionnaire to these incumbents.
4. Identify those items which are answered differently by the long tenure group versus the short tenure group or the high performers versus the low performers.
5. Cross-validate by administering to another group of incumbents those items which differentiate the low group from the high group to see if the validity identified in the previous sample holds up.
6. Place the cross-validated items into the selection system (usually no more than 20 or 30 of the 150 items will survive).
7. Score the candidate's responses to these items to determine the probability of high performance or tenure.

Before we leave the area of testing, it should be pointed out that some people are better test takers than others. Often a candidate would make an excellent sergeant or captain but freezes up on the tests. This is certainly a reality of the whole testing field and is further complicated by the fact that minorities tend to do less well on paper and pencil tests than the nonminorities.

It is suggested that this non–job-related influence on the test scores be reduced when possible by offering a pretraining program to people who are considering the police profession. This could take many forms, but one possibility is a brief session covering different types of tests and such basics about testing as being careful to read the directions, spending initial time on questions which one can answer quickly and not spending a lot of time on one item.

Sample tests and practice on a similar test are also useful (certain test publishers have such pretest instruments on the market). When possible, advance notice of the general content and format of the tests is also recommended. Certainly we see this in promotional paper and pencil tests where a reading list is given out prior to the examination.

There are two types of selection models. The first model is called the *successive hurdle* model. It is based on the idea that there are certain minimal standards of each component that each person must reach. If they do not reach this minimum, they do not pass on to the next component. An example of a successive hurdle would be speaking and understanding the English language. If a person cannot understand English he does not pass that particular hurdle and would be eliminated as a patrol officer candidate.

The converse model is labeled the *compensatory* model. The assumption here is that low performance in one component, rather than eliminating the candidate, can be compensated for by high performance in another area. An example would be a particular candidate who does not communicate well verbally but is extremely hard working and generally gets along well with people around him. In a compensatory model, the rationale is that high performance on other KSAPCs compensates for lower performance on the skill of verbal communications.

In many cases, both selection models are used within one selection system. However, one should recognize what type of model one is using with a particular predictor component.

Combining Selection Component Scores to Generate a Final Eligible List Score

A number of the selection components, such as the medical examination, will be administered on a pass/fail basis. This involves what was previously referred to as the successive hurdles model. Those people who make it through the hurdles will have a group of scores in such things as paper and pencil tests, background information, training and experience.

Typically, different weights are assigned to different selection components such as 40 percent for the oral board, 40 percent for the paper and pencil tests, and perhaps 20 percent for background data. The weights to be assigned should be determined by the importance and number of KSAPCs which a particular component measures. If the oral board is measuring seven of the top ten KSAPCs for the job and the written test is only measuring two, then one will probably place more weight on the oral board.

One other consideration in assigning weights is how effective and sound the selection instrument is. If the interviewers for the oral board are poorly trained, this would tend to offset the advantage described above.

Whatever weights are assigned, the scores of each component should be converted into Z or T scores so that they can be combined with one another. If you have three predictors and two of them show little variation, you should consult a local statistician for ways to correct for restriction of range. If you do not, you run the risk of putting too much weight on the one predictor that has a great deal of variation regardless of the percentage assigned to the particular predictor.

The percentage of weighting assigned to a given predictor can be entirely negated by the restriction of range problem. Consider the situation in which ten candidates for police sergeant are being evaluated and time as a patrol officer is one of the predictors along with a paper and pencil test. If the maximum number of years allowable is five, and nine of the candidates have more than five years, then their score would be five and one candidate's score would be four years. Assuming that the test scores range from 70 percent to 100 percent, we now have two sets of scores for the ten candidates. Let us also assume that we decided to place a great deal of weight on experience. So we assign 90 percent to experience and only 10 percent to the paper and pencil test score. One can see that, because of an extreme restriction of range problem, the ranking on the list would be decided almost entirely by a paper and pencil test score despite its 10 percent weight. Since almost everyone is identical in experience, the only variation possible is in the testing score. This type of restriction of range problem makes it imperative that one anticipate the problem before the predictors are administered and seek out ways of increasing legitimate variation among the selection scores.

The oral board or interview is the most frequently used selection component. (Some studies estimate that 99 percent of the decisions to hire in the United States today are preceded by some sort of interview.) Yet it is one of the most difficult selection components to validate.

The reason for the frequency of use is obvious. It is common sense to interview a candidate before you select him.

There are many reasons for the validation problem, including the poor training of interviewers and the lack of awareness of what one is trying to gain in the interview. Many people go into an oral board to "just chat" with the candidate and get a "gut impression." While there is nothing wrong with obtaining a gut impression, an interviewer should have a clear picture of the job-related qualities desired in an applicant before he goes into the interview. These qualities should be clearly defined, taken from the job analysis list of KSAPCs, and put on a rating form which can allow the interviewer to rate the person immediately after the interview. All of these issues are treated in a brief volume entitled *Interviewing for the Decisionmaker* by Lawrence R. O'Leary (1976b).

Once the interviewer is clear regarding what he is looking for, it is helpful to develop a basic list of questions to be used. One general rule in forming this list is to use an open-ended question format. The purpose of the oral board is to allow the candidate to generate behavior which the interviewers can use to rate him on a number of job-related scores. If the interviewer asks very limited questions such as "Did you like your last job?" which permit only yes or no answers then he is reducing the amount of behavior which can be observed. The same question can be asked in an open-ended way which will encourage the *interviewee* to do much of the talking. Such a question could be "Tell me about your last job."

The basic sequence prior to and during an interview should be as follows: (1) Identify and explicitly define the KSAs to be measured in the interview (see Appendix H). (2) Interviewers should prepare for the interview by becoming familiar with the candidate's background data before beginning the interview. (There is nothing more irritating than being asked questions that you have already answered on your application form.) (3) During the interview the interviewer should treat the candidate in a way that he would want to be treated. (Do not make the mistake of believing that being very formal and official makes one more objective or impartial. In fact, it may turn off candidates to the point that it causes them to "clam up." This will directly limit your ability to gather information.)   (4) After allowing and encouraging them to talk about topics they are interested in, direct the interview toward the job-related issues (KSAs) that you plan to cover through the use of open-ended and nonleading questions. (5) Probe areas that cause questions in your mind and *that are job related.*   (6) Terminate the interview only after giving a clear understanding of what will happen next to the candidate. (E.g. he will be notified by mail or he must report to Room 245 for an eye test at 8:30 AM next Thursday.)   (7) Rate the candidate immediately after completion of the interview. (A delay here almost invariably leads to a reduction of a clear impression of the interviewee's behavior and in many cases a blurring with the behavior of another candidate.)

Training Oral Board Members

It is my belief that the many errors committed in the police oral boards are actually exceeded by the extent of the errors made prior to convening the board. One of these errors is a failure to define and concisely state the KSAs to be measured in the oral board. This has been previously discussed. However, a second point needs to be mentioned and that is the importance of interviewer training.

Oral boards are all too frequently conceived by simply passing out a general rating form to the members who have all just arrived, frequently with little awareness of what makes a sound interview. Any time from a half hour to two days of interviewer training (KSA definition, rating errors, probing, fair employment issues, skill practice sessions) is time well spent prior to the oral board.

Monitoring the System

All too often, selection systems are installed and not reviewed for the next fifteen to twenty years. They are changed only when complaints get so loud that something must be done. A better way to proceed would be to set up a monitoring system for periodic review of the selection program—say, once or twice a year.

There are two types of monitoring systems. The first type is an immediate kind which breaks down the selection system into stages and identifies total numbers of people going through each stage from initial application through placement on the police force as a permanent employee. At each stage, not only would the total number of people arriving at that stage or predictor component be listed, but percentages of minorities and females would also be listed. Such a flow sheet can give management not only a picture of the numbers of people arriving at a particular component of the selection system, but also serve as an early warning as to any component which may have an adverse impact. In some cases, it may be legally acceptable (i.e. if it is the only job-related method of selecting candidates), but if it is having an adverse impact, management should be aware of it and continue to use it only with full knowledge of its problems and the reasons for continuing it. (See sample flow chart in Figure 3.)

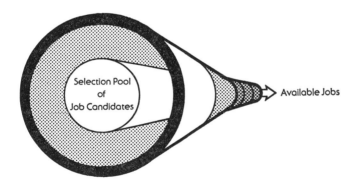

THE SELECTION PIPELINE

Figure 3.

The second type of monitoring will occur over a longer time span. In those cases where large numbers of people have passed through the selection system, have been selected and subsequently put in a job for a substantial period of time (i.e. in excess of six months), a classical concurrent validity study can be conducted

by collecting performance measures on these candidates and correlating that with the predictors previously collected.   However,
this sort of validity study usually takes more than a year or two to
initiate because sufficient numbers are not hired immediately
thereby allowing the study to begin six months after the testing.

Chapter 6

FAIR EMPLOYMENT PRACTICES

B Y ITS VERY nature, the selection process is one that is going to be challenged. The act of selecting involves a process of choosing one or a few from among many. Seen from the other perspective, it is excluding many by picking only a few. Although most people can see the logic and the necessity of making such a selection, the very process and the sound of the words, "picking a few from among many" do not seem to fit well in the same sentence with such democratic phrases as "we are all created equal" and "everyone has an equal chance."

Even without the whole issue of discrimination against minorities and other protected classes, *the whole process of selection has an aroma of elitism* that will *never be completely eliminated.* The best that can be hoped for is an understanding of the logic and rationale behind the selection system. Under the best of circumstances, those commodities are not in abundant supply among people who have not been selected.

When you combine that situation with the history of discrimination in the world and the friction generated in this country when our democracy has tried to correct the effects of past discrimination, you have an even more complicated situation. I will try to address the problem and provide a recommended solution; but before I do this, I think it is important to organize some of the many legal events that have changed the selection process dramatically in this country. The same principles such as the use of the systems approach in selection and the establishment of job relatedness still apply. In point of fact, they apply even more because of these legal events or at least their application is even more critical because there is suspicion, friction, and discrimination. Therefore, the selection process that is used must include job-related and consistent standards against which each candidate for the position can be evaluated.

As we proceed with our brief history of fair employment legislation, the reader is encouraged not to forget the above point.

Fair Employment Legislation

In 1964 a law was passed which has come to be known as the 1964 Civil Rights Act and it guaranteed equal housing opportunity, equal educational opportunity, and equal employment opportunity to minorities. Title VII of that act focused on the equal employment phase of the legislation and resulted in the creation of a federal agency known as the Equal Employment Opportunity Commission. This agency was to examine complaints of unlawful discrimination by minorities and assist the complainant in pursuing his cause through the judicial system. The commission, in turn, drew up guidelines for selection procedures published in 1964 which gave employers some idea of what their selection systems should look like. The act was subsequently amended in 1972 and included public employers under the purview of the Equal Employment Opportunity Commission (EEOC). In addition to this agency and its guidelines, there were other federal agencies focusing on fair employment issues. These include the Office of Federal Contracts Compliance Programs (OFCCP) which focused primarily on organizations holding federal contracts and the Civil Service Commission, dealing primarily with the public employment sector. To further complicate the picture, there are state fair employment agencies as well as large municipal agencies dealing with fair employment issues.

Although the EEOC guidelines on selection systems were legal guidelines that were based on the professional guidelines embodied in the APA *Standards on Educational and Psychological Tests* (1966), there were some significant alterations including the prioritization of criterion-related validity in terms of desirability over the other validity models mentioned in the APA standards. Because of some of the inconsistencies in the enforcement of the guidelines and some professional disagreement with the emphasis on criterion-related validity, the Equal Employment Opportunity Coordinating Council, which is composed of the Department of Labor, the Equal Employment Opportunity Commission, the Civil Rights Commission, the Civil Service Commission, and the Department of Justice, was charged by law to eliminate inconsistencies among the operations of the agencies and departments responsible for enforcement of federal equal employment opportunity law. "Pursuant to that mandate, the Coordinating Council began work on proposed uniform guidelines on employee selection procedures early in 1973" *(Federal Register 41,* No. 227). The EEOC subsequently decided not to accept these guidelines and refused to endorse them. However, the Justice Department, the Department of Labor, and the Civil Service Commission did form the Federal Executive Agency and endorsed the guidelines formulated by the majority of the old Equal Employment Opportunity Coordinating Council and labeled them FEA "Guidelines on Employee Selection Procedures."

Since the implementation of the 1964 Civil Rights Act, there has been a very substantial number of court cases dealing with organizations applying unlawful discriminatory employment practices.

I do not believe that a description of many or even a brief sample of these court cases would accomplish much in this book. In fact, I believe it would detract from the overall objective of the book which is to give the reader a firm grounding in the consideration of the steps to take in generating a sound selection system.

However, I would like to take a few moments to focus on a couple of court cases that have historical importance and briefly touch on the thrust of many of the court decisions and what they are looking for. Historical court decisions include a number of the Supreme Court decisions such as the *Griggs v. Duke Power* case in which Chief Justice Burger's Supreme Court ruled unanimously against Duke Power and its misapplication of a number of standardized tests and other selection procedures. There was an obvious misuse of testing in this case but it is also important to note that Chief Justice Burger, in writing the court's opinion, emphasized that this was not a decision against testing but rather against the misuse of tests.

A second landmark case was that of *Albemarle v. Moody* (422

US 405, 425). This was another Supreme Court case in which the court found the Albemarle Paper Company guilty of discrimination in their hiring procedures and emphasized the importance of the EEOC's guidelines in coming to their decision.

The final case to be mentioned here is the *Davis v. Washington* case. In that case, tried before the Supreme Court, the Washington, D. C. Police Department was charged with discriminatory practices in selecting its entry level patrol officers. In this case, the Supreme Court attempted to establish more balance in the enforcement of the 1964 and 1972 Civil Rights Acts by emphasizing the equality of the content validity model with that of the criterion-related validity model. It also alluded to the acceptability and, in fact, did accept the performance of probationary patrol officers in the academy as one criterion for success on the job.

The Thrust of Court Action In the Fair Employment Field

Anyone who reviews the transcripts of court cases in the fair employment field and more specifically the basis on which decisions are made can readily see that the federal judges frequently attempt to make their decision on the legality or illegality of a particular selection procedure. This is accomplished by examining its adherence to professional standards in developing a selection system (e.g. the APA *Standards on Educational and Psychological Tests*) and secondly on the degree of adverse impact that a particular component of a selection system has.

This term, "adverse impact," is an important one for the whole fair employment area, so a moment should be spent discussing it. Adverse impact occurs when the rate of selection is much lower for a protected class than it is for the rest of the population. More specifically, the FEA guidelines generally regard adverse impact as "a selection rate for any racial, ethnic, or sex group which is less than four-fifths ($^4/_5$ or 80%) of the rate for the group with the highest rate."

The concept of adverse impact is also important because the selection systems that have adverse impact are the specific ones that the federal guidelines are aimed at eliminating. The FEA guidelines call for generation and presentation of validity evidence on those selection systems having an adverse impact. Strictly speaking a department would not be required under the FEA guidelines to produce validity evidence on a selection system which did *not* have an adverse impact on protected classes. It would be a poor organizational decision not to attempt to check on the validity of such a major selection system, but it is not demanded by law involved in the fair employment guidelines.

Reverse Discrimination

One exception to this general rule might be a court imposed quota system which did not discriminate against minorities but required that a certain percentage of all new people hired be members of a protected class. Such court imposed solutions involving quotas have triggered counteractive suits by nonminorities. The latter's contention has generally been that their rights have been violated by giving the job to a minority member who did less well on the selection system than they did.

The field of fair employment is generating a reduction of blatant discrimination cases. In many of the court cases, it is becoming increasingly difficult to tell the good guys from the bad guys. This is particularly true when it comes to adherence to quota systems.

This was never clearer than in the *Defunis v. Washington* case. That Supreme Court case involved a college graduate (Defunis) who had applied for law school at Washington State University. His admission test scores (LSAT) and his college grades were quite high. They were so high in fact that the university, which was filling its quota of minorities established by its own affirmative action program, passed over him to pick the highest scoring minority applicant. When he took the case to court, they ruled in one direction and the appelate court reversed the lower court's decision. The Supreme Court agreed to hear the case, and the stage was set for the highest court in the land to speak on this very complicated issue.

My point in narrating this case is found in the Supreme Court's decision in the Defunis case. The complexity of the issues is reflected in the fact that the Supreme Court of the United

States, supposedly containing some of the most experienced and talented legal minds in the country, dealt with the issue by deciding not to decide in the case. By the time the decision was to be made, Defunis had been admitted to law school and was about to graduate, so the Court said the point was moot. Similar cases will continue to arise and eventually force the Court to make a decision which will add a slight amount of clarity. Meanwhile police departments are being asked to make these decisions because manpower requirements demand that selection continue on some basis. This is not an easy position to be in.

Recruitment

Throughout the book the importance of beginning the development of a selection process with a job analysis has been emphasized. Up until now, I have been guilty of a slight oversimplification. It is true that the job analysis is a start and that then one begins to examine how he is going to measure the qualities that the job analysis indicates are important for this specific position. However, there is a parallel effort that actually needs to occur simultaneously with the development of measuring devices to put into the selection system.

Once the KSAPCs have been established, the selection specialist should not only work on developing sound selection components but begin giving very serious consideration to the whole issue of recruitment. The importance of this component of the selection system cannot be overemphasized. Its centrality is put in perspective by a comment made frequently by some test experts in describing the whole system of selection. "You can't put in manure and come out with roses."

The whole selection system could follow the *Standards on Educational and Psychological Tests* exactly with the exception of this recruitment component and the system would be very ineffective.

There appears to be two fundamental components to any successful recruitment program. The first of these is to identify what the significant qualities are and the population to whom you want to appeal (e.g. college graduates, junior college graduates, high school graduates, returning veterans, blacks, or females) and to develop a strong recruiting program to reach these groups. The second component involves developing an organizational impact on the community that maximizes the probability that recruitment probes into these different publics or employment pools will result in a positive reaction. In other words, the first component focuses on getting the question asked of the right people; the second component focuses on increasing the probability that their response will be favorable.

Recruitment is important and, in fact, is essential as a component of any successful selection system. In some cases, an organization may have the luxury of many of those people who have the KSAPCs for the position coming into the organization and seeking out the position. In most cases this is not true and the organization is required to seek out the desired population.

Recruitment is important in any selection system but perhaps more important in those where the organization is attempting to overcome a previously existing adverse impact in their selection system. The topic has been talked about before but it is not uncommon to recognize an underrepresentation of minorities or other protected classes in the work force and then to begin one's selection audit and see that some of the greatest adverse impact is in "getting members of the protected classes in the door to apply for the job." It is true for blacks and it is also true for females in many areas.

A substantial part of the underrepresentation of the minority group members in this country's law enforcement field is due to some of the requirements of selection procedures that have been used in the past which have not been related to the job. These include the use of standard paper and pencil tests which have a built-in cultural bias and a very distant relationship to the prediction of a successful performance as a police officer. However, an equally important component of the crop has been the reluctance of minority group members to seek out employment with law enforcement agencies. Much has been written about this problem and it is not an objective of this volume to get deeply into the sociological and psychological aspects of the origins of this unfortunate reality.

However, it is productive to examine the reality and ask ourselves the question, "Where do we go from here?" Probably there was no point in time in this country's history when the antagonism between the law enforcement agencies and the minority populations was greater than during the riots of the 60s. One part of the attempts to deal with that problem was put down on paper by a blue ribbon panel including such people as Senator Edward Brooke, Mayor John Lindsay, Roy Wilkins, I.W. Abel, and, the chairman, the late Otto Kerner, then governor of the state of Illinois. *The Kerner Commission Report* (1968) is a very thick volume containing an examination of many facets of the riots of the 60s. The document also attempts to make very specific recommendations regarding solutions to some of the specific problems identified.

The statistics gathered at the time indicated that out of approximately 80,621 police officers taken from a cross section of major municipal departments from across the country, 7,046 were nonwhite. This represents less than 10 percent of the police force sample where as the percentage of nonwhite population in these same cities is well over 25 percent. The report goes on to say "there are even more marked disproportions of negro supervisory personnel. Our survey showed the following ratios: 1 in every 26 negroes is a sergeant, the white ratio is 1 in 12; 1 in every 114 negroes is a lieutenant, the white ratio is 1 in 26; 1 in every 235 negroes is a captain or above, the white ratio is 1 in 53."

Specific recommendations included "police departments should intensify their efforts to recruit more negroes. The police task force crime commission discussed a number of ways to do this and the problems involved . . . in order to increase the number of negroes in supervisory positions, police departments should review promotion policies to insure that negroes have full opportunity to be rapidly and fairly promoted."

One thing is clear, the effects of past attitudes are not only going to call for an organizational commitment to actively seek out and recruit minority group members for police positions but also to take concrete steps to eliminate any procedure which unfairly impedes the career progress of minority group members. In conversations with a minority recruit officer from a major metropolitan department, this latter effort was described as critical. He pointed out that it was imperative that an organization be able to point to progress in not only minority representation in entry level positions but especially in the supervisory jobs as a key component for attracting more minorities to apply for positions within that organization.

Finally, it should be emphasized that no selection system is going to cure this problem by itself unless the organization is committed to doing whatever needs to be done in order to attract and recruit candidates from all facets of our society who have the potential to do the job. These are the built-in blocks that are just as necessary for a sound selection system as a well-done job analysis.

One Recommended Solution

The fact of the matter is that the fair employment issue must be dealt with directly by close adherence to sound selection procedures. This includes not only a review of every selection component in the system to establish its job relatedness by following the procedures outlined in the previous chapters of this book, such as job analysis, but also by doing a systematic selection audit.

A selection audit is achieved by reviewing past records of applicants for a specific position and identifying which of those were members of a protected class and which were not. This is the pool from which the job incumbents were selected.

A sample of a selection audit is included in the Appendix I but would involve looking at each step of the selection process from inquiries about the position to completing an application to the preliminary interview or screening interview to the next phase in which candidates are screened in or screened out all the way through until the final oral board before being hired or being promoted. As you can see by looking at the example, at each selection point the total percentage of people screened in/screened out is calculated as well as the percentage for certain classes and the percentage for the rest of the group. Such an audit can serve to easily identify which components have an adverse impact.

If a component does have an adverse impact, the agency must decide whether there is another way to measure the KSAs that they are identifying in that particular component. If there is and it is feasible, then they should seriously consider using it. If there is not, then the development of some type of validity evidence should be planned and implemented. A third possibility is to modify the existing component having adverse impact to try and reduce that impact while still keeping the component.

Basically, my view is that the fair employment legal events (legislation and court cases) have spawned two broad classes of solutions: (1) the "job-relatedness" solution and (2) the "job-relatedness-plus" solution.

The *job-relatedness solution* recognizes the fact that there has been discrimination in the past and contends the solution is *to begin now and use a job-related selection system*. This solution interprets "fair employment" and "equal employment opportunity" as meaning establishing a job-related selection system and hopefully having no adverse impact. If there is a selection system that is equally valid and has less or no adverse impact, this solution would advocate using that approach.

The *job-related-plus* (JRP) solution contends that the job-related solution is too little. More specifically, the JRP solution emphasizes the point that an implementation of the job-related solution will not be enough because of past discrimination. JRP further contends that the implementation of the JR solution will provide for such a slow assimilation of the protected classes that it will be decades before the representation of the protected classes in the entry level of the work force will approximate the percentages of the protected classes in the selection pool.

The JRP solution further contends that the job-related solution will require an even longer and intolerable time frame for the protected class representation to reach acceptable levels in the supervisory, mid-management, and top management levels.

The JRP solution contends that quotas, goals, and time-tables are necessary to counteract the effect of past discrimination. Critics of the JRP solution contend that it will lead to charges of reverse discrimination. Others say it is no solution because it simply substitutes one form of discrimination for another.

Whatever the solution, there must be an appreciation of two needs: (1) that of the department to have job-related standards on which to base its selection system and (2) that of the protected classes to be assimilated throughout the departments in numbers consistent with their representation in the selection pool. The courts have imposed quotas to assist in addressing the second need. However, even in the *Griggs v. Duke Power* case, as well as in all the federal guidelines, great pains have been taken to preserve the employers right to select on a job-related basis.

The fair employment issue may come into better focus if the reader recognizes that a selection system can be rated on two dimensions: (1) validity (Does the system select successful people?) and (2) cultural fairness. The ideal would be a system which was both highly valid and high on cultural fairness (i.e. little or no adverse impact).

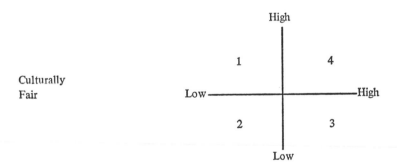

These would be found in Quadrant 4. Quadrant 3 would represent the quota solutions which have low validity but high "cultural fairness." Quadrant 1 represents tests that are valid but low on cultural fairness (have an adverse impact).

This type of selection system is legal if there is no "more culturally fair" alternative. An example would be a reading test which is job related because the reading skill is necessary not only on the job but in getting through the academy. Such a selection component is valid, job related, and can be used. However, steps should be taken to reduce the existing adverse impact.

Quadrant 2 represents those solutions that have low validity and little cultural fairness. Many of the omnibus intelligence tests for success in entry level positions including police officer fall into this quadrant.

The future solution will depend on our ability as a society and the technical hardware of the selection field to effectively mold validity and cultural fairness in the same selection system. Whatever the solutions of the future, this country will not be improved by selecting people exclusively on non–job-related qualities.

Chapter 7

SELECTION AND PROMOTION

U P TO THIS POINT, we have talked about the selection system in general, the importance of defining the job in specific terms, and fair employment. Now we enter another area of selection, the promotion decision, which I see as sufficiently different from the entry level issue to generate a separate chapter. Before getting into these differences, let me point out that the decision to fill a promotional position such as sergeant or even colonel should be followed immediately by a thorough job analysis similar to the one at the entry level position. The process of selection is meaningless when one does not know what he is trying to predict.

A job analysis can be conducted using the incumbents in the position and the superiors of that position, if possible, in developing the tasks and the KSAPCs required for that specific position. However, when it comes to the selection system used in promotion, the components of the system should be somewhat different from the entry level. For example, qualities such as planning and organizing, leadership, the ability to delegate responsibility, management control, and decisiveness may not be unique to the management or supervisory position but certainly become more and more important in the supervisory role. The ability of the paper and pencil test or the interview to measure the management skills just mentioned is severely limited. The most important disadvantage of the interview in promotional situations is that *there is very little relationship between the behavior required in the interview and the behavior required on the job.* As a result, there are many areas in which the interviewee can hide in an interview. We usually speak of this person as the candidate "who talks a good game."

A second problem is the fact that many interviewers are poorly trained and therefore are easily distracted into a discussion of irrelevant issues. One captain for a major metropolitan police department told me that virtually all of his interview time for promotion to captain was taken up discussing his activities as a high school football player. While there is nothing wrong with touching upon a candidate's sports activities, the discussion of that topic to the exclusion of all others is a distortion of the selection interview.

Even if the interview was theoretically a good selection tool, the problem in implementing it is a serious one. The implementation phase can obviously mean the difference between a sound selection system and a completely invalid one. That statement is obvious but bears saying, especially when one has seen departments with selection programs which are excellent on the drawing boards but for one reason or another simply cannot be effective. One state has dropped the oral board from its selection system simply because of an implementation problem. Rather than implement it poorly, they elected to discontinue it.

In addition to the problem of knowing specifically what the position calls for, other widespread problems in promotional procedures are (1) overstressing the importance of job tenure or seniority, (2) an oral board with members who have little knowledge of the position for which the board is being convened (e.g. a captain of the state highway patrol serving on the board to evaluate candidates for a metropolitan police department with quite different job responsibilities), and (3) paper and pencil tests which are not related to the job in question and also have an adverse impact.

If the department decides to keep the tradition of the selection procedure of written tests, oral board, and some extra points for seniority and perhaps education, I see nothing wrong with administering such job-related tests as a reading test since the amount of material they will be reading will in all probability be increased in a supervisory position. The reader is already aware of my reservations regarding the traditional model (e.g. written test or oral board). More specifically, the traditional model produces information on specific knowledge areas (e.g. general orders or local ordinances) and what the person says about himself. Actual job-related behavior displayed in the interview is quite limited (e.g. oral communications, dress, listening skills). This topic will be discussed further later on in this chapter. Though it has selected many competent officers, the interview has also selected people who are markedly unqualified for the job. One of the reasons for these selection mistakes is the lack of sufficient job-related behavior to observe prior to promoting the candidate.

Is there a better way? If a department wanted to improve its selection program for key positions in the management level of the organization, how would they go about doing it? How does a department get sound, objective, job-related, and culturally fair measures on such qualities as supervisory skills, management skills, delegation, management control, planning and organizing, problem analysis, leadership, decisiveness, and judgment?

One answer is a promotional procedure which the author has installed in a number of law enforcement and public safety agencies across the country including the Kansas City (Missouri) Police Department, the Rochester (New York) Police Department, and the Mississippi Bureau of Narcotics. Fire departments such as the St. Louis Fire Department have also used this approach for top management selection. The procedure has been adopted recently by the Federal Bureau of Investigation for their field office supervisor positions. A number of other police departments, including the International Association of Chiefs of Police, have also utilized this approach.

The method is known as the *assessment center.* It was developed at Harvard University in the 1930s and was subsequently utilized by the German military command in World War II and also by the Office of Strategic Services (OSS). Very simply, *the assessment center is a series of job simulation exercises which are designed to generate job-related behavior.* In 1958 it was installed and then its effectiveness as a selection tool was evaluated in a study of supervisors and managers within the American Telephone and Telegraph System by Douglas Bray, chief psychologist for that organization.

The evaluation was called the "Management Progress Study." It involved the processing of over 200 college graduates and non-graduates who had been hired through the assessment center. Reports were written on the employees and then locked up for eight years. The reports were opened at that time and comparisons were made between the predictions and actual job performance. In this carefully controlled study, the assessment center results were found to be highly valid and quite effective in predicting supervisory effectiveness. In fact, it was even more predictive of success at higher levels of management.

Since that time, such private corporations as IBM, Sears Roebuck and Company, Standard Oil of Ohio, J. C. Penney Company, and General Electric have installed assessment centers for management level positions within their organizations. Many of these companies have evaluated the effectiveness of the assessment center with essentially the same results as the "Management Progress Study." Much of this research has also identified the assessment center as being culturally fair. In most instances, it has not created an adverse impact and, in almost all instances, it has been job related. In recognition of this success record, the EEOC recommended the assessment center as *the* method for assessing the management potential of female employees who had alleged past discrimination in promotion.

As stated previously, the problems with the oral board are that there are many places to hide in an interview and there is little relationship between what the candidate is asked to do in the interview and what he is asked to do on the job. Consequently, the interviewer is forced to make his judgment based on what the interviewee *says* rather than what he *does*. In contrast, the assessment center requires the candidate to perform activities which are job related. These exercises are generally broken down into three categories: (1) individual exercises, (2) one-on-one exercises, and (3) group exercises.

INDIVIDUAL EXERCISES: For example, one of the principal activities of a captain in a police department is to review and take action on written documents which cross his desk. These take many forms. It may be a vacation schedule, a letter from the wife of a subordinate complaining about the hours and asking that her husband be transferred to a different shift, directives from the captain's superior asking him to look into specific instances of reported misconduct by the men in his command, or a request by that same superior to provide a special squad of officers for an upcoming rock concert to be held in a local arena (see Appendix E). Thirty such items are developed and put into an envelope with an explanation of the exercise and what is expected. The candidate is given an organizational chart showing to whom he reports and who reports to him in this upcoming exercise.

For the next three hours the candidate is required to review this material (referred to as an in-basket), take some action, and designate in writing what that action is. The candidate has many options, including decisively dealing with the issue at that time, gathering more information, delegating it to someone under him, or a combination of these. However, he must write down what he plans to do. After the testing period is over, the material is returned to the envelope and labeled with his name. It is subsequently given to an assessor who has been trained to evaluate this material. The assessor reviews it and identifies specific documents which the assessor may have some question about. An in-basket interview is scheduled and during that interview, the assessor or observer (the terms are synonomous) queries the candidate about his reasons for taking certain actions. The reasons behind the action can be as important as the action itself. Note that this exercise is "a piece of the job."

Another example of an individual exercise is one labeled the problem analysis exercise. Typically, a specific problem with a good deal of technical data is handed to the candidate and he is given a few hours to review it and come up with a document which is his solution to the problem. If the candidate's ability to stand up and make a presentation to a group is an important ability for the captain's position, that can be incorporated into the assessment center as well.

ONE-ON-ONE EXERCISES: A significant skill for many supervisors and managers is the ability to coach and counsel a subordinate in a one-on-one situation. The ability to conduct this type of interview is critical in many supervisory and management positions. Consequently, an exercise called interview simulation is frequently found in an assessment center and involves the candidate playing the role of a sergeant or captain who has a subordinate whose performance is less than desirable. The specific problem can vary, but the exercise involves the candidate playing the role of the superior with a trained role player playing the role of the subordinate and the observer or assessor doing nothing more than just that—observing and assessing. It should be noted that during this observation time, the observer has been trained to simply record behavior.

Another example of a one-on-one exercise is labeled the fact finding exercise. Many supervisors, sergeants, lieutenants, and captains are quite good at their job because they know how to dig for information. How often has the reader made a decision based on inadequate information and later wished he had dug a little deeper first?

The fact finding exercise measures this ability by presenting a problem such as this: "You are the personnel director of a department, just recently appointed, and a subordinate requests funds to continue an attitude survey within the department. Your predecessor turned down that request before he left the position. Your objective is to make a decision regarding the request.

"To help you in that decision, a resource person who has many facts regarding the situation will be willing to answer any question you want to ask for a period of fifteen minutes. Once that period is over, you are to render a decision which must be approved or not approved because the budget must be submitted shortly. After your decision, the resource person will ask you a few questions and provide you with some information you may have missed to see if that will change your decision." The candidate is given five minutes to prepare his line of questioning, then proceeds to question the resource person and is told to make his questions more specific if he asks very general types of questions. After he gives his decision and the reasons behind it, other information is given to him to see if he will be swayed from his original position. Key skills such as fact gathering, planning and organizing, stress tolerance, and decisiveness are measured in this particular exercise.

GROUP EXERCISES: Another significant portion of the manager's activities is performed as a member of a group, in either directing the group or participating as an equal. Consequently, leaderless group discussions are included in the assessment center and involve the candidate's participation in small group discussions of approximately six people. The physical setting is a room having a round table with six candidates sitting around the table. Also in the room but seated away from the table are three assessors who do not take part in the actual exercise. Again, their sole function is to observe and record behavior. An administrator reads the directions including the objective (which usually is to reach a group agreement and approve a written list of recommendations on problems confronting the department). After that time, the candidates have approximately one hour to reach a group decision.

These group discussions can be of two varieties. If a candidate is simply a member of a task force without individual roles, then the leaderless group discussion is labeled "nonassigned role." If, on the other hand, the group is made up of members each of whom is assigned a specific role, the group is then known as "assigned role."

The assessment center method also contends that the people best qualified to judge the performance of candidates for the position are the people who have reported to that position, have worked in the general climate of the department, have worked in the target position, and who now supervise that position. No one is better qualified and more knowledgeable about that job. Although many will agree with this, some will say, "Yes, but if certain people that I know were selected as assessors for sergeant position and they are now captains, they would assess their friends as being more competent than people who were unknown to them." This is the very reason why there are checks and balances put into the assessment center system. As you go through the system, you will see how any attempt to give extra credit to a friend will be minimized, if allowed at all.

Once the KSAPCs have been identified and weighted according to their importance to a specific target position, the specific exercises for the assessment center will be developed. These are the exercises which will generate the most job-related behavior for the specific dimensions to be measured. Typically, each dimension is measured in more than one exercise so that if you have five exercises you may have three independent measures of problem analysis as well as three independent measures of planning and organizing, etc.

The assessment center can be run in many different ways, but a typical one might have 12 participants being considered for a target position of police sergeant. As you will see this type of program can be implemented so that many more than 12 people can be evaluated. In Kansas City, 117 sergeant candidates were processed through an assessment center. The assessment center would be held as the final selector and would typically involve some kind of prescreening device such as a paper and pencil test, as used in the Kansas City assessment center, or some other approach to reduce the overall number of candidates.

One of the reasons for this need to reduce the overall number is the requirement by the assessment center method that there be one assessor for each two participants. So if there are twelve participants in an assessment center, there should be six assessors. Once trained, these assessors can be used over and over again to process a large number of candidates, but the two to one ratio is widely accepted by assessment center practitioners.

Subsequent to the identification of exercises (some of which can be developed and tailor-made for the department, others of which can be purchased from assessment center publishing houses such as Development Dimensions, Inc. in Pittsburgh), the assessors will be chosen from the target position's supervisors. If the target position is sergeant, then the assessors would be picked from among the lieutenant rank. If a few captains must be included, it should be done in such a way that the lieutenants feel free to speak.

A schedule for the assessment center is established including the training period. Typically, on Wednesday, Thursday, and Friday prior to the assessment center week, the assessors are brought in and trained by an administrator. They are instructed in how to observe behavior and what to observe. They are also instructed to record everything and they are given a schedule as to which candidates they will observe in each exercise. The assessment center is so structured that assessors observe different participants for different exercises. This negates the possibility that one particular candidate may be rated poorly throughout the assessment center because he has the same assessor who does not like him for some reason or another. As a result, each candidate is observed by as many as three or four assessors independently.

Another part of assessor training is the viewing of videotapes of exercises in which they practice recording behavior after which their performance is critiqued by the administrator. They are also trained in interviewing candidates and getting practice in doing that as well. The tenor of these assessor training programs is usually very serious because most assessors realize that they are dealing with a person's career.

The actual assessment center can last anywhere from one to three days. Typically, the time during which the participants are at the center is longer for more responsible, higher level jobs such as captain or major than for first line or middle management positions.

The beginning of the assessment center is marked by an introduction by the administrator explaining the assessment center, he should be open with the candidates, encouraging them to become involved, and participating in the exercises. Candidates are given an opportunity to ask questions and encouraged to stay on schedule. Schedules are very important in the assessment center because exercises must begin and end on time.

After the candidates have gone through the exercises, they are asked to rate their reactions to the different exercises and to the assessment center. They are again given an opportunity to ask questions. One of the questions asked frequently is do they get feedback. Most assessment centers do generate a final report which lists the candidate's major strengths and two or three of his major areas of developmental need. The department can elect to provide this feedback to the individual, reviewing the report with him on a one-to-one basis, or they can forego such feedback as too time-consuming. I encourage such feedback whenever possible because it gives the person who can do something about his weaknesses the information he needs to begin.

After the participants have left, the assessors score their exercises. This involves reviewing the observations they have recorded and classifying that behavior into a particular quality or dimension. They might include such things as the following: "John interrupted Tom seven times during the course of the group discussion"—classified as poor listening skills. "For forty minutes of the leaderless discussion group, John looked down at the table even when he was talking to others"—poor impact. "John picked up the implication of committing $20,000 of the department's funds for new cars in terms of the problems it would create in diverting those funds from an area of higher priority need"—good problem analysis. "John initiated seven recommendations to the group regarding action they should take"—good decisiveness. This process occurs not only for one exercise but is performed by each assessor for each exercise.

Subsequent to that classification, the assessor then assigns a number, usually from one to five, for the overall rating of a specific dimension for a specific exercise. After classifying all the behavioral observations into different dimensions and indicating whether they are positive or negative, the assessor would then review his form, review all of the positives and negatives for a specific quality, and decide what rating to assign for that exercise. Consequently, at the end of this process, each assessor has scored each dimension for each exercise.

Now comes the final major portion of the assessment center—the assessor discussion. It involves the examination of all the behavioral observations made for one candidate and a discussion of those observations by every assessor who saw that candidate. If the assessment center involves five exercises, there may be anywhere from three to five assessors who saw the candidate. If there are less than five assessors, obviously one or more of them has seen the candidate twice. The candidate is the focal point of this discussion and all of the assessors come to this assessor discussion with the scored forms for only that particular candidate.

The discussion usually begins with the assessor who has seen that candidate in the background interview going over his background and then reviewing the dimensions which he has rated based on that interview performance. For example, he would list motivation and state the rating which he gave this person on motivation. For example if the candidate's name is Jerry King, he would say, "Jerry received a five on motivation for these reasons . . ." and he would list the plusses and minuses which would be the behavioral observations recorded for motivation.

If some of the other assessors disagree with the rating, they could question the rating or point out that perhaps some of the behaviors that the assessor had included under motivation might be better located under a different dimension. In any case, there is discussion among the assessors.

At the end of the discussion, each assessor rates the candidate for motivation, then the interview assessor goes on to the next dimension and repeats the process. Next, he would sit back and allow another assessor who had Jerry King in the leaderless group discussion go through the same process for that exercise. All along, each assessor is recording the ratings for each dimension given by the other assessors and his own rating based on what he has heard from the presenting assessor. Sometimes these ratings will be quite similar, sometimes they will be slightly different. If they are markedly different, assessor discussion should occur. Typically, this activity is overseen by an assessment center administrator, as I have done frequently.

At the end of the assessor discussions, each assessor has a listing of ratings for each dimension. This listing will be made up of ratings received from each exercise so that the dimension of planning and organizing will have a rating from the in-basket exercise, from the background interview, from the leaderless group discussion, and from the fact-finding exercise. The assessors would review all four of those ratings and come up with an overall rating for that particular dimension and would record that on the assessor discussion form for each of the dimensions in the assessment center.

Finally, the overall ratings assigned to each of the dimensions would be listed on a flip chart. Since there are three or four assessors there will be three or four columns of figures for each dimension. These ratings are made independently and once they are put up on the flip chart, the administrator along with the assessors examine the ratings and discuss any differences (e.g. three of the assessors may have rated Jerry King 4 on the problem analysis and one rated him 3). When there are differences, a brief discussion is held to see if a divergent assessor feels comfortable in changing his rating. He does not have to change; in some cases an agreement cannot be reached and those four scores are averaged. The final product of the assessor discussion is a list of scores, one for each dimension in the assessment center. These are then weighted according to their importance in the job analysis and the weighted scores are totalled.

It should be pointed out that the assessors do not know the weights assigned to the different dimensions. This is done to avoid the bias which might result from such knowledge.

The final product of the assessment center is a total weighted score on which an eligible list could be based. It is important to know that that weighted score is based not only on key job-related factors but also reflects the relative importance of each of those factors. That weighted score can then be combined with other predictors such as paper and pencil tests to come to an overall score.

I have administered assessment centers in which hundreds of candidates have been evaluated. A description of the assessment center process would be incomplete if I did not describe the pervading attitude of the assessors. It can best be described by one assessor's comment and it is a highly consistent attitude from assessor to assessor and from center to center. "If I was a participant, I would want the assessors to give me their best shot; so by God, I'm going to give my best effort to them (the participants)."

As mentioned before, the assessment center can provide a feedback report as well as strengths and weaknesses on all of the dimensions listed in the assessment center. This can provide some interesting benefits for the police department. First, it can identify specific developmental needs within the department. This can be used by the training department to develop training programs aimed directly at the needs within the department, rather than broad-brush training programs which frequently do not address the specific needs within the department. A second advantage to getting measures on specific KSAPCs is unique to police departments. Say that a departmental director has two or three candidates for a position in the investigative unit for sex crimes. While the three candidates being considered had the same overall scores in the assessment center, one candidate's scores in the area of fact-gathering, problem analysis, and impact and sensitivity are much higher than the others. This is useful information in making his decision.

Another benefit involves the acceptability of the assessment center process. Every assessment center with which I have been associated has been regarded by both participants and assessors as the most job-related method of selection they have ever seen. It should be pointed out that these comments are made anonymously.

Finally, there are spin-off benefits of the assessment center such as the increased effectiveness of the assessors at interviewing and rating their own people at performance appraisal time.

An example of one department's implementation of the assessment center process might help to clarify the working of the assessment center within the police agency. The following description of the steps taken in implementing the assessment center for the ranks of sergeant, detective, and captain in the Kansas City Police Department was published in the IPMA Publication *Public Personnel Management* in November/December 1976.

The program described here is, of course, neither a complete replacement of paper and pencil tests nor a flawless alternative. It is, however, a systems approach substantially different from and more job related than mere oral board and paper and pencil testing. There are various ways in which a typical assessment center can be implemented. The following was not atypical and should give the reader a flavor for what is involved.

Over a period of two years, in excess of 250 candidates were evaluated in the Kansas City Police Department assessment center for three separate positions — sergeant, detective, and captain. The problems associated with selecting sergeants from a police department's pool of police officers are like those involved with selecting any other first-line supervisory personnel. They are reflected in the many variations of the following comment frequently voiced by people who have passed promotional tests as well as by people who have not: "It's really a shame that someone like John Smith will never make sergeant when he has all the qualities of a good sergeant, but simply doesn't do well on a written test." This problem has plagued police departments for years.

In addition, measuring the supervisory and administrative skills for any first-line supervisory position is more difficult than measuring specific knowledge areas (e.g., general orders, investigative procedures, etc.). Paper and pencil supervisory tests are almost always transparent and can be successfully completed by people who are good test takers but who are not necessarily good supervisors.

Selecting the best patrol sergeant candidates is particularly critical because the position itself is of such great importance in the effective discharge of the department's duties. Now it has become even more important since federal agencies are withholding revenue sharing and other federal funds pending the department's demonstration that their selection and promotion procedures are job related, valid, and culturally fair. When the Kansas City Police Department was confronted with the task of generating an eligibility list for the position of sergeant, Dr. Joseph MacNamara, chief of police, and Major Marvin Van Kirk, director of the Bureau of Personnel for the department, selected a three-step procedure as the selection process. This follows a systems approach to selection that avoids too much reliance on any one tool.

Phase I involved a paper and pencil test covering a specific amount of job-related material, which was contained in a limited number of books available to all the candidates. This test was examined by a consultant to determine the cultural fairness of the items prior to the administration of the test.

Phase II was a candidate review board involving a review of each candidate's personnel file. This phase was to determine whether any of the captains on the review committee knew of any significant reasons a specific candidate should not be considered for the third selection process. Consistent disciplinary problems, drinking, etc. were the types of factors for which the committee would rule out a candidate.

Phase III was the implementation of a job simulation approach to selection, the assessment center. Because the assessment center was considered to be highly job related, a departmental decision was made to give as many candidates as possible an opportunity to go through this phase. A total of 117 candidates were evaluated in the sergeant's assessment center for the latter half of 1974.

One of the basic attractions to the Kansas City Police Department was the capacity of the assessment center's exercises to be developed in such a way as to closely mirror the duties and responsibilities of the patrol sergeant. The one-day exercises required the candidate to display behavior that could be observed and measured by a number of trained assessors. This is quite different from evaluating the candidate's response to a series of paper and pencil questions, which can only measure the knowledge of a series of facts or what a person says he or she would do in a given situation.

The actual assessment center was conducted in the Kansas City Police Department only after the skills and abilities required for the position of patrol sergeant were determined through a series of job analysis interviews with people who were currently in the target position of patrol sergeant. A series of exercises was tailored to simulate many of the duties and responsibilities of this position. Each candidate proceeded through all the exercises of the day, and his or her performance was observed by different trained observers for each exercise. This provided multiple ratings on nine different key dimensions previously identified as important to the position of patrol sergeant. The observers were selected from the rank of captain because those people were in a key position to judge the adequacy of performance for the position of patrol sergeant. This was true because all of them had personally (1) reported to that position of sergeant at one time, (2) previously performed in the position of patrol sergeant, and (3) were currently supervising that position. Moreover, the twenty observers spent two days in intensive training designed to enable them to make objective and standard recommendations based on observed behavior.

Other factors that maximized the objectivity of the ratings involved not only the use of multiple raters or observers for each participant, but also gathering measures from multiple exercises before the final measure on a specific quality or trait was determined by the observer group. Even then, the observers had to justify their ratings to the other observers who had watched the same candidate in different exercises.

Finally, any observer who had supervised the specific candidate within the previous year was asked to disqualify himself or herself as an assessor for that candidate. In many cases, observers would spontaneously disqualify themselves for these reasons before being asked to do so.

The philosophy characterizing the entire project was one of encouraging a systematic and representative input from those presently in the position of patrol sergeant to determine what tasks were important and, consequently, what skills and abilities would be required for the job. Sergeants Troy Majors and Tom Mills of the Kansas City Police Department were very helpful in developing materials for the assessment center and maintaining a close liaison between the project director and the department.

In a day when the job relatedness of different selection procedures is being closely scrutinized, it is important to consider how job related the participants and observers in the Kansas City assessment center felt the procedure was. To this end, an anonymous participant and observer questionnaire was handed out to members of the two groups with the purpose of obtaining their honest evaluations of the program. The participants were asked, "To what extent do you think the assessment center was job related for the rank of sergeant?" The responses received indicated a high degree of acceptance:

To a very great extent	47
To a great extent	52
To some extent	4
To a slight extent	0
To a very slight extent	0

The reactions of the assessors were equally positive in response to the question, "How much reliance should a supervisor put on the results of the assessment center?"

A very great deal	2
A great deal	13
A moderate deal	2
Not much reliance	0
No reliance	0

The results of the assessment center were combined with the written test to generate a final score used to develop the eligibility list. It should be pointed out that management was quite pleased to see a large degree of variance in the scores of the assessment center, thus avoiding a frequent problem in selection occurring when all of those being tested or interviewed are clustered together in a large group at the end. The degree of variation can be seen in Table I.

TABLE I

Category	Mean	Standard Deviation
Final weighted score	76.45	12.69
Reading comprehension	71.01	22.50
Reading speed	68.45	21.90
Written test	17.74	1.34
Age	31.76	5.24
Tenure	6.97	3.88

Table I. Means and Standard Deviations for Selected Variables on the Sergeant's Assessment Center.

The Kansas City Police Department is currently engaged in efforts to use the assessment center for a number of other positions (i.e., efforts have been completed and assessment centers run subsequent to the sergeant assessment center for the position of detective and captain). However, one may wonder about the validity and/or cultural fairness of the assessment center. Federal agencies will rarely, if ever, say that a given procedure is valid or that a given test is job related in general. However, if one examines one of the largest settlements signed by the EEOC — namely, the AT & T consent decree which involved $46 millon — one will find that the EEOC identified and agreed to the use of the assessment center as part of the solution to past discrimination. In addition, a study done at AT & T under the direction of Dr. James Huck examines the fairness of the assessment center to minorities and women. His basic conclusion, using the assessment center results, was that the procedure is, in fact, culturally fair and fair to women.

These findings were supported in the Kansas City assessment center for sergeants, although the promoted people have not been on the job long enough to permit a criterion-related validity study at this time. Some preliminary statistics are available now, however. Pearsonian correlations were computed between key scores involving the assessment center. The results of this analysis and the significant correlation beyond the 0.05 level are reported in Table II.

The Successful Police Officer

TABLE II

	Final Weighted Score	Reading Comprehension	Reading Speed	Written Test	Age	Education	Tenure
Final weighted assessment center score	N.S.	N.S.	N.S.	N.S	N.S.	0.19	N.S
Reading comprehension			0.90	0.23	—0.37	0.21	—0.42
Reading speed				0.21	—0.41	0.28	—0.50
Written test					—0.20	0.22	—0.26
Age						—0.20	0.73
Education							—0.35
Tenure							

Table II. An Intercorrelational Matrix for Selected Variables.
N.S. = Not significant at the 0.05 level

Of the 117 sergeant candidates attending the Kansas City Police Department assessment center, 6 were members of a minority group. Although this is a statistically small sample, it is interesting to note that the average weighted score for minority group members was slightly higher than average for the 111 white candidates. The 1 female who participated in the sergeant's assessment center scored above the average for the total sample on the final weighted score.

Other interesting statistics include substantial negative correlations between time on the job and such measures as the reading test and the written test. This is consistent with a general tendency on the part of older people to perform less well on paper and pencil tests than younger people. In contrast, the assessment center was not significantly correlated with time on the job, thus dispelling any fear on the part of the participants that they would be at a disadvantage because they are inexperienced or too old. The lack of a significant correlation between written tests and assessment center results suggests that the two instruments are measuring two different factors. This is as desired since if there were a strong correlation between the two, the question would arise as to whether both the test and the assessment center were needed. The assessment center measured something untapped by paper and pencil tests in this situation.

The procedure in the Kansas City Police Department has been considered job related, culturally fair, and content valid. Previous studies in other organizations have demonstrated the validity of the methods, and current research is underway to examine the long-range effectiveness of the sergeant's assessment center. In addition, there is very substantial interest in the assessment center's future use in identifying the specific developmental needs among people in top management positions. These will then be used as one of the basic components on which to build both training programs and career paths.

The captains who were involved in the program certainly believe the assessment center was effective both selectively and developmentally. This is very much in evidence in the anonymous responses to the question, "Would you send one of your subordinates to the assessment center?"

Yes, definitely	16
Yes, probably	1
Can't make up my mind	0
No, definitely	0

One other indicator of the assessment center's acceptability by those using it is its expanded use in other positions within the department. Since the sergeant's assessment center, the Kansas City Police Department has run an assessment center for the positions of detective and captain. In the latter assessment center, the participants were evaluated on five different exercises during a period of two days. This allowed five independent evaluations of the candidate's behavior on five job-related exercises.

Some of the captains and majors who served as assessors in the captain's assessment center expressed an interest in participating in an assessment center themselves. They were interested in obtaining an objective feedback on their own career development. This appears to be the next direction the Kansas City Police Department will take in continuing to use the assessment center.

Well-meaning public employers who are becoming more and more sophisticated in the test validation area may very well want to consider the possibilities offered by the assessment center. Today, there is an ever-increasing number of selection specialists, such as Dunnette and McClelland, who are advocating a more substantial inclusion of job-related and behaviorally oriented predictor components. As mentioned before, after critically reviewing a good deal of research on paper and pencil testing in predicting job success, David McClelland drew the following conclusions:

The best testing is criterion sampling (job simulation). The point is so obvious that it would scarcely be worth mentioning if it had not been obscured so often by psychologists like McNemar and Jensen who tout the general intelligence factor. If you want to know how well a person can drive a car (the criterion), you test his ability to do so by giving him a driver's test. Do not give him a paper and pencil test for following directions, a general intelligence test, etc. As noted above, there is ample evidence that tests which sample job skills will predict proficiency on the job.

Academic skills tests are successful precisely because they involve criterion sampling for the most part. The Scholastic Aptitude Test taps skills that the teacher is looking for and will give high grades for. No one could object if it had been recognized widely that this was all that was going on when aptitude tests were used to predict who would do well in school. The trouble started only when people assumed that these skills had some more general validity, as implied in the use of such words as intelligence. Yet, even a little criterion analysis would show that there are almost no occupations in life situations which require a person to do word analogies, choose the most correct of four alternative meanings of a word, etc.

Criterion sampling means that testers have got to get out of their offices where they play endless word and paper and pencil games, and get into the field where they actually analyze performance into its components. If you want to know who will be a good policeman, follow him around, make a list of his activities, and sample from that list in screening applicants. Some of the job sampling will have to be based on theory as well as on practice, but what is called for is nothing less than a revision of the role itself — moving away from word games and statistics toward behavioral analysis.

Obviously, this is going to take years and years, but it eventually must come. In mountain climbing, you are taught that you must move away from the face of a cliff in order to more effectively plant your feet in the small footholds that you eke out of the mountainside. Public employers are confronted with a very difficult mountain climb called fair employment. Anyone who has worked in the field for any substantial period of time knows that there are very few easy solutions to these problems. Federal legislation such as the 1972 Civil Rights Act and subsequent court decisions have motivated some employers to take increasing action in the fair employment field. However, it has made others more cautious about even sincere and honest attempts to improve their selection systems.

These employers must recognize that dealing successfully with the mountain is going to require moving away from its face to seek out additional ways of improving their selection systems. Those predictor systems which increase the amount of predicted job performance variance are the only reasonable alternatives to the quotas most employers and the general public find difficult to accept. However, this will only come when the objectivity bias is diminished, enabling the right of the employer to choose who he is going to hire or promote to be matched by the employee's right to be selected or deselected by job-related predictor systems.

This article's title raised a question: Can we have both objectivity and job relatedness? While the two characteristics of a valid selection device appear somewhat incompatible at first blush, certain job simulation procedures (such as those found in many assessment centers) hold out an opportunity for selection specialists to dramatically increase their selection systems' job relatedness. This increase can be obtained without substantially reducing the important quality of selection objectivity.

In summation I would like to point out that this is just one application of the assessment center and that the method is quite flexible and can be used in many different situations. For example, in the Rochester (New York) Police Department there were no specific knowledges to be tested when the candidates were being considered for the investigator position. Consequently, the in-basket exercise was modified to become a case file which the investigator candidate was to examine and review before compiling a document which would list the steps he would take to complete the investigation. That document then was reviewed and discussed with the candidate by one of the assessors who were investigative sergeants with the department.

Interestingly enough, the department agreed to my recommendation that in lieu of an objective written test, the case file would be part of the screening program to determine who would go to the assessment center. This is unusual and probably the first attempt to take the in-basket or its equivalent out of the assessment center and move it ahead into the selection process to be a screening device. This was done with the recognition that the in-basket is probably one of the more influential components of the assessment center.

If one is interested in more information about the assessment center refer to Marvin Van Kirk's *FBI Journal* article on the Kansas City Assessment Center as well as Bill Byham's *Harvard Business Review* article on the assessment center. Based on the benefits of the assessment center, the basic common sense of the approach, and the increasing need to select competent management personnel, I predict that the assessment center will be a rapidly growing approach to management selection and development in the near future.

Obviously, the working test period should be implemented in the selection system for a promotional position as well. Hopefully, after the assessment center and the working test period, there will be few being deselected, but that working test period still should be considered a true test.

For years management in many law enforcement agencies have looked at the whole process of selection as "frustrating trivia." The process was considered trivia because it was not directly related (or at least not apparently so) to reducing crime, reducing costs, or improving the public relations image of the department as a whole. It was frustrating because there were no methods of selection which were far more effective than other methods. Most departments have used some form of written test and oral board. So things have gone pretty much the same from department to department and there has been a resignation to the fact that "selection and promotion of officers is a fuzzy area."

As has been demonstrated in previous sections of the book and in this chapter, there are clearly better ways of dealing with the selection decision. However, there is no magic in the selection system. It is only as good as the effort and knowledge put into it. Perhaps my predecessors have been partly responsible for conveying the image that "psychological tests" and "psychiatric examinations" in some way magically identify substantial portions of that population who would have trouble if they became police officers or were promoted into management within a police department. No doubt there is an area of emotional pathology which the psychiatric and psychological examinations can pick up which might have gone undiscovered by lay people. However, that is quite different from relying on those types of reports which tell if "this candidate would be a good police officer" or "this candidate would be a good police captain."

If positive change is going to occur in the selection systems in the law enforcement agencies in this country, it must be preceded by three events: (1) Top management in law enforcement agencies must recognize the need for change. (2) That same management must also recognize that there is a better way and that the better way can be implemented within their department. (3) Management must agree that the better approach to selection requires more time and money than the previous approach.

Event 1 has occurred in many police agencies. Event 2 is just beginning to occur in some agencies and has not begun in others. There are still many departments which prefer the traditional way of hiring and promoting people, saying, "It was good enough for us when we were coming up the ranks" or "It isn't perfect, but no system is." However, Event 3 is the one which will determine whether police agencies improve their selection procedures.

I have examined at first hand the characteristics of good managers within many departments. Many characteristics are listed as indicators of a good manager such as planning and organizing, delegating, and even developing his subordinates. Rarely, if ever, has his effectiveness in selecting people for the department been listed as a measure of a good manager. Selection of competent people for the department *is* as crucial as many other commonly agreed upon indicators of a successful manager.

An improved selection system will not occur in a police department if top management is not thoroughly committed to that improvement and willing to (1) communicate that commitment up and down the line and (2) provide the financial and personnel resources necessary to implement the new selection procedure.

From the time the Mississippi Bureau of Narcotics introduced the assessment center process into the law enforcement field by evaluating its field agents for supervisory positions, the process has enjoyed a substantial degree of success. The police departments in New York City; Kansas City, Missouri; Rochester, New York; and the Federal Bureau of Investigation have further spearheaded its implementation within the law enforcement field. Since then, other city departments as well as the Missouri Highway Patrol have extended its use within the field.

Other agencies within the judicial system, such as probation and parole agencies as well as correctional institutions could use the approach for selecting and developing people to fill supervisory and administrative positions. I have also used it to fill high level positions (chief and deputy chief within the St. Louis Fire Department). The method is a sound one and will be around for a long time to come. This is mainly due to the increasing realization that selection systems, if they are to be developed, should be developed correctly.

Chapter 8

REVIEW AND SUMMARY

A FEW MONTHS ago I addressed a professional group on the topic of interviewing. Someone had asked me to bring a copy of a book that I had written on the subject and when a member of the group looked through the book he noticed my wife had underlined a number of sections that she thought were particularly important. The reader jokingly asked me, "If you underlined the important points, does that mean that the rest of the book is unimportant?"

Having completed this volume I now feel somewhat the same in picking areas for review and summary. An author always feels that almost all that he has put in the book is important or else he would not have put it in. I will try to mention only a few major concepts that deserve reinforcement from this whole field of selection in law enforcement.

The objective of this book has been twofold. The first was to render the selection field "interpretable" by developing and presenting a basic conceptual approach to effective selection. Many organizations lack that basic conceptual approach even though they recognize that effective selection is an important ingredient of any police organization. The organizations that do not have a sound conceptual idea of where they are going in terms of selection are characterized by fragmented efforts to run out and grab this new test or that quickie approach to selection. First, one has to translate the objective of getting the best people for the job into an obtainable and logical overall plan. This is the "job analysis to selection plan to selection components to monitoring the system model" that has been described in the book.

The second objective was to go beyond just the development of a selection process and the need for an overall plan by providing the basic tools necessary to begin and in some cases complete the development of an effective selection package within the law enforcement field. The discussion of basic topics in the glossary of terms as well as some of the fundamentals in statistics is designed to provide the user with some basic information about the method of approaching the development of the overall selection program, as well as each component. I have taught many people in the area of developing selection systems and I have always been impressed with the eagerness and thirst for information that many people within an organization have. It has been difficult many times to accept the existence of this eagerness when the paltry amount of training that is given to these people is considered.

This volume is an attempt to give those people who day in and day out have to make selection decisions and set up systems on which these decisions are based, some additional tools to help them upgrade those selection systems. These people also need support from society and their supervisors because they work in a difficult field which generates a lot of resistance on the part of the people who come into contact with them. In addition to all the obvious negative reactions that they get because they are eliminating many people from consideration (some state highway patrols have in excess of 30,000 applications for a few hundred positions), there is an eliteness or at least an exclusive connotation to the whole process of selection. The personnel worker should recognize that this problem is present but also recognize that it is absolutely essential that a selection decision be made and be made on a job-related basis. It is not only top management's responsibility but also top management's right to select personnel on a job-related basis. If the performance of the people in the organization deteriorates and is not at an acceptable level, the people who screamed about the selection system and the fact that they were excluded are not going to be held accountable. The public will hold top management accountable. With the responsibility of effectively discharging the law enforcement services of the community goes the responsibility of picking people that can most effectively do the job.

Anyone working in the selection field should recognize that fair employment is here to stay and rightfully so. One has to constantly be aware of the potential problem of adverse impact.

There is a twofold question involved with this problem: (1) Is the selection system and each component job related? (2) If it is and it has an adverse impact, is there some alternative way of measuring those particular job qualities which would have less of an adverse impact?

If the law enforcement agencies in this nation move in the direction of basing selection decisions on non–job-related qualities exclusively, the quality of work in this country, as well as the morale of the American worker, will deteriorate sharply. Hopefully this volume has not only identified an alternative but, just as importantly, has given some specific directions on how to achieve that goal.

In the previous seven chapters an attempt has been made to examine some very important and difficult decisions facing every law enforcement organization in this country. No attempt has been made to pinpoint a specific test or a specific selection device as one that everyone should use. Instead, the basic components of both the decision and the method of making the decision have been detailed for the reader (i.e. (1) analyzing the specific job, (2) identifying the specific KSAs required by that position, (3) developing a logical selection plan which is psychometrically sound, and (4) monitoring the system to minimize selection errors and modify the selection system to improve its validity).

Treatment of such topics as basic statistical concepts were included because I believe that top management within law enforcement agencies and certainly the personnel administrators within those agencies should have a familiarity with these concepts if they are going to make enlightened decisions in these areas in the future. Additional topics that are equally critical but may be readable only by the test specialist include item analysis and a more elaborate discussion of the concept of adverse impact, both of which have been discussed in appendices in this volume. These were placed there to afford the reader the opportunity to read on those topics if he so chooses, but does not want to delve heavily into those areas.

The need to select effective police officers is not going to decrease in the future. The pressures of our society are going to require that the selection of these people be given even further attention than they are today. Consequently, the law enforcement administrator and supervisor who participates in this process is going to have to be familiar with many of the concepts addressed in this volume. I predict that the use of the assessment center for promotional decisions will significantly increase in the future. As has been mentioned before, this will be due to the realization that the procedure is not perfect but at the present time is the most job-related and valid method of selecting supervisors and administrators available to us.

The information, concepts, and ideas presented in this volume are an attempt to increase the predictive effectiveness of the selection systems that organizations develop. Those systems have to be based on and closely tied to the specific qualities identified as necessary for the position in question. Even when this is done, prediction errors will not be totally eliminated. As was mentioned at the beginning of this volume, selection errors will always be with us but a sound selection system can help to reduce their frequency. You should not use that fact as an excuse but should remember it to prevent yourself from repeatedly throwing out selection approaches simply because they have resulted in an error. Such a move is a mistake because there are no error-free systems.

Appendix A

THE NEED FOR QUANTIFICATION

I F THE PREDICTOR system is going to evaluate candidates along job-related lines and the system has more candidates available than jobs, then that evaluation is going to have to involve some kind of ranking or categorization of candidates regarding their probable success on the job. Let us consider the following example:

Assume that we have 5 sergeant positions open and we have 100 candidates. A typical procedure in the law enforcement field would be to give a sergeant's written test followed by an oral board. However, the need for quantification becomes apparent when one tries to imagine analyzing the results of the selection system without some sort of quantification. To simply say John Jones got some questions right on the test and some questions wrong on the written test and he seems to be pretty knowledgeable about municipal ordinances but less knowledgeable about departmental rules and that he did pretty well on the oral board starts to communicate why we need some kind of quantification. The quantification must be there in order to permit comparisons of one applicant to another or one group of applicants to another group.

It should be acknowledged at the outset that there is a general tendency in many people to resist quantification. This resistance comes partly from a feeling that quantification of people is dehumanizing and/or people are too complicated to be quantified. Actually there has been justification for this feeling in the past. When a large group of candidates, say 150, who are seeking the position of sergeant take a written test and all the candidates score within four or five points of one another, it is very difficult to have useful quantification. In such a situation, a decision to use such a paper and pencil test as the sole predictor or even the major predictor of who becomes sergeant suggests that people who had a point or a half a point higher score than others would be better sergeants. This is a very questionable assumption at best and is a corner that selection personnel should not get themselves backed into.

Under these conditions, it is no wonder that critiques of testing accuse the test creators and selection system developers (psychometricians) of being pseudoscientists. This problem is known as restriction of range and is a problem to be both aware of and to avoid at all possible costs. This procedure creates such situations as the following which occurred in a major municipality a number of years ago. The mayor of a large municipality was accused of favoritism when he planned to promote a friend of his to a high level commissioner position. His defense was to publicly state, "I will appoint the man who scores highest on the civil service test for the commissioner's job." When his man came in second by 0.086 of a point he appointed the top scorer and called the Civil Service Department to tell them, "You cut the bologna pretty thin over there, don't you."

The solution is not to throw out quantification. In the foreseeable future, there is going to be a very definite need for quantifying information. The answer is to make the statistics on numbers being applied to selection systems serve your purposes by quantifying more realistic factors. This is not as difficult as it sounds, but does require a blend of logic (using a job-related systems approach) and some basic knowledge of sound testing procedures and statistics.

In the mechanics of dealing with a group of people each having one or more scores, it is important that we acknowledge the fact that some kind of number has to be assigned to a person if we are going to ultimately wind up with an eligible list. You can use scores that are very gross, such as the upper third of the group or the lower third of the group, or you can use very specific numerical scores. The advantages and disadvantages of each approach will be discussed later. It should be pointed out at this time that the remainder of this appendix will include some practical examples of some basic statistical procedures. These are presented to increase the reader's awareness of these procedures and demonstrate that there is nothing magical about statistics.

There are two major concepts about group data that should be kept in mind. One is that any group of data such as a group of heights of people in a classroom or a series of test scores on that same group will tend to cluster around a central point. This phenomenon is called central tendency. The second quality of all distributions (which is a group of data) is apparent when one recognizes that all scores of our hypothetical group of heights *are not identical.* If they are not identical then they vary, they are different from one another. The amount of variation of these scores is important as we will see later. How much they vary is reflected in a number of scores—some common, some not so common. This quality of a distribution is known as variance. In sum, we have two major qualities of distributions: (1) central tendency and (2) variance.

Let me point out at the beginning that we are going to get into some very basic aspects of quantification. These will be helpful to those dealing with predictor scores on a day to day basis. Before starting with a discussion of these basic aspects, let us consider a group of data (typically called an array or a distribution) that represents a list of written test scores on a promotional procedure for sergeant's position within a metropolitan police department: (Figure 4 consists of 40 scores on a sergeant's promotional test.)

80	74	58	49
76	80	49	57
62	78	54	89
40	60	52	71
80	92	62	74
84	91	67	74
86	80	61	80
91	79	88	92
84	62	90	87
62	75	49	65

Mean = 72.1   Standard Deviation = 14.17

Figure 4. Data Array

Central Tendency

The first concept is a fairly simple one and hopefully it is apparent that one very communicative number can be given about an array which will describe that group of data to someone who is unfamiliar with it. It would be the average or mean of that group. The two terms, average and mean, are synonymous.

There are a number of symbols used in statistics that should be labeled here:

X = raw score
Σ = sum of
N = number of scores in array
X̄ = average
x = deviation score
SD = standard deviation

These symbols are common in statistics and will be used in the rest of the appendix. Therefore, the arithmetic mean or average is equal to ΣX divided by N. The mean is the most commonly used measure of central tendency and representative of an array of scores in many cases. One of the problems with the mean as a measure of central tendency is that it is influenced by extreme scores. To demonstrate this problem assume that you returned to your old high school for a ten-year reunion. A questionnaire is passed around and you are asked to put down your annual salary; these salaries are averaged across the twenty people attending the reunion. Let us also assume that three of the people were very fortunate and had a good deal of money so that their annual income was $500,000 each. The remaining seventeen had incomes that ranged from $7,000 to $20,000.

Under these conditions, the average income for the people attending the class reunion could probably be near $30,000 or $40,000. Yet this average score is not representative of the group as a whole. The reason for the distortion is the mean's sensitivity to extreme scores.

One way to get around this is to ignore the absolute quantity of the scores and just rank the scores from highest to lowest and count down to the middle or median score. This will give us the median which is that score in the distribution or array which divides the group of scores into two equal halves. It is literally the middle score. (It is interesting to note that computation of the median involves treating the scores like internal data, that is, the scores are larger or smaller than other scores but the size is not important.)

In our example, we would count down to the person having the tenth score and because there are an even number of scores, we could interpolate between the tenth and eleventh scores and call that our median. Since our three affluent high school graduates would all be considered as just a number (i.e. ranks one, two, and three) they would not effect the computation of the median. In these circumstances, the median would in effect be somewhere around $13,000 or $14,000 and in this example representative of the center of distribution. Whenever your distribution of scores suffers from a substantial number of extreme scores that are quite extreme and particularly when they are exclusively in one direction (e.g. very high scores or very low scores) then one can consider the median as more representative of the center of distribution.

A final measure of central tendency which is not very commonly used because it is the most crude of the central tendency measures is called the mode. The mode is simply the most frequently occurring score in the distribution. In many cases this score is near the center of the array of scores. In the array of data provided, the most frequently observed sergeant's test score is 80. It is around the center of distribution, and therefore can be considered a measure (although crude) of central tendency.

Variation

As previously mentioned, scores are not identical in a distribution, therefore they vary. The amount of this variance or spread of scores is equally important for the test expert to know. There are three measures of variation, with the last one being the one most commonly used. They are the range, the average deviation, and the standard deviation. The range is simply the highest score minus the lowest score plus 1. In our distribution of scores above, we can say the range of the scores on the sergeant's promotion test was 92-40 + 1 which equals 53.

If one were reviewing the results of the sergeant's test a week after the list was posted it might be communicative to someone who is not familiar with the test to be told that the range of scores of the test was 53.

The *range* is a very simple concept to understand and a simple statistic to compute. Like most things that are simple and easy to do, there are a number of problems with the range. The major problem is, like the mean, the range is susceptible to extreme scores. Let us examine the problem in the example of the listed incomes of our twenty high school graduates. Assuming that the highest reported income was $500,000 annual income and the lowest was $7,000. The range would be $500,000 minus $7,000 or $493,000. This reported range implies a great deal of variation among the scores when this may very well not be true. In point of fact, seventeen of the scores varied less than eight or nine thousand dollars from one another and many of them are even closer together than that.

One way around this problem is to measure how far each individual score deviates or varies from the average. All of the scores are added up and the average is computed. This average $(\overline{X})$ is then subtracted from each of the raw scores (X). The result is what is called a deviation score (x). Therefore, $x = X - \overline{X}$.

If one then sums these deviation scores and takes the average, the result will be zero. The reason for this is that the deviations above the mean will equal the deviations below the mean, and when you sum them it will come out to be zero. This is not a very communicative statistic. One could deal with just the absolute values of the deviations (ignore the sign of the deviation) and then come up with an average, but there are some problems with this also.

Consequently, the best measure of variation is called the standard deviation. This simply takes the deviation scores mentioned above and squares each deviation score (x^2). These squared deviation scores eliminate the sign of the deviation. When added up, this gives the sum of squared deviations (Σx^2). This is then divided by the number of scores and we come up with a statistic called the variance, which is symbolized by S^2. If the square root of that variance is taken, we come up with a statistic known as the standard deviation $(SD = \sqrt{S^2})$.

Normal Curve

What does it tell us to know that the standard deviation of an array is 14.17? To answer this question, we have to talk a little bit about a concept called the normal curve or bell-shaped curve. A lot of mathematical activity has centered around the bell-shaped curve. Consequently we know a great deal about it. Fortunately, we do not have to go into the mathematics of that curve very deeply. There are a couple of things that one must accept with faith if one is not going to go into the mathematical derivations and demonstrations.

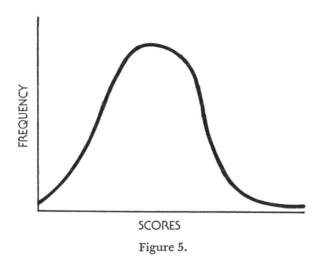

SCORES

Figure 5.

The bell-shaped curve or normal distribution is shown in Figure 5. Imagine a graph with the scores on some dimension or quality (e.g. height, IQ, age, annual income) along the horizontal or abscissa value of the graph. The vertical or ordinant value of the graph represents the number of people in that sample having that particular score. For example, the average IQ in the population is set at 100. So 100 is the midpoint or average of this distribution.

As you can see by simply examining the bell-shaped curve, its highest point (or the score most frequently occurring) is toward the middle and as you move away from the middle on either side there are fewer and fewer cases. This is simply a graph representation of a phenomenon we see every day. If a group of people come together for a specific purpose and you simply ask them to indicate their heights on a piece of paper, then you would find that there is an average height and that most people in your group (particularly if it is a large group) will be around the average and as you move away from the average in either direction, fewer and fewer people have those heights.

Mathematicians tell us a couple of things about the bell-shaped curve. First, they can identify a point on either side of the average which represents one standard deviation above the mean and one standard deviation below the mean and tell us that essentially 34 percent of the sample of scores will fall between the mean and this point of one standard deviation above the mean. An additional 34 percent will fall between the mean and the point which is one standard deviation below the mean (see Figure 6).

Secondly, they tell us that an additional 14 percent will fall between that point identified as one standard deviation above the mean and a point identified as two standard deviations above the mean. The same is true for the interval between one and two standard deviations below the mean, namely that 14 percent will occur in that interval.

Let us take an example of an array of data presented earlier in the appendix and compute the standard deviation before returning to our original question of what does a standard deviation of 14.17 really mean.

The first thing that we should keep in mind when going from the normal curve to a specific distribution like the sergeant's test is that every distribution has a specific value for its average and a specific value for its standard deviation. Those are the two quantities obtained from the specific distribution. These quantities can then be plugged into the normal distribution. In Figure 6 you will see a normal distribution or bell-shaped curve with the mean or average in the middle and the standard deviation lines marked cutting off the percentages previously described.

Remember that 34 percent of the scores or distribution can be found between the average and one standard deviation above the

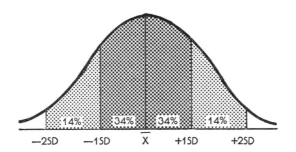

NORMAL CURVE SHOWING MEAN AND SD DISTANCES

Figure 6.

average. An additional 34 percent can be found between the average and one standard deviation below the average. Consequently, 68 percent of the distribution can be found between the value equivalent to one standard deviation below the mean and one standard deviation above the mean. Similarly, 96 percent (68% + 28% = 96%) of the population can be found between the values of two standard deviations above the mean and two standard deviations below the mean. Finally, almost 99 percent of the sample can be found between the values of three standard deviations above and below the mean. Because the tails of the curve never reach the abscissa value, there is always mathematically a few cases outside of any cutoff that you want to make.

Obviously, if you were to graph the values in the sergeant's test it might not be as smooth as this bell-shaped curve. However, as you add values and get up to quantities of 100 or 200 or 1000 the graph will start to assume a smooth configuration.

The second step in the pursuit of the answer to the question of what does the standard deviation of 14.17 mean would be to add our specific sample values into the bell-shaped curve.

This is shown in Figure 7.

As you can see, the values for this sample's standard deviation have been added and subtracted from the mean so that now we can say that 34 percent of the scores lie between the mean and 86.27. We can also say that 68 percent of the cases fall between

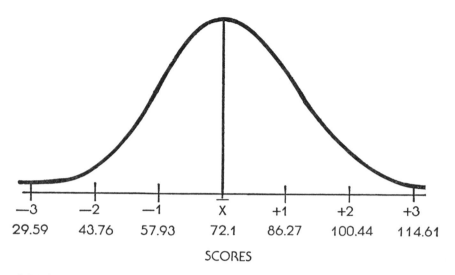

| −3 | −2 | −1 | X | +1 | +2 | +3 |
| 29.59 | 43.76 | 57.93 | 72.1 | 86.27 | 100.44 | 114.61 |

SCORES

DISTRIBUTION CURVE SHOWING MEAN AND SD DISTANCES

Figure 7.

the values of 57.93 and 86.27.

Now one can see that the question of what does a standard deviation of 14.17 really mean can be given two immediate answers. First of all, the larger the value of the standard deviation the more spread out the scores will be. That is, a distribution having a standard deviation of ten has scores spread out more than a distribution having a standard deviation of four.

Secondly, one can take the value of the standard deviation, add it to the mean and get one value, or subtract and get another value. Only 70 percent of the scores in the sample fall between those two values. Some other significances of this will be seen in the very near future. Generally in testing you want to generate as much variance and get the standard deviations as high as possible. This idea will be further developed later, but is mainly due to the fact that a constriction of scores around a central point makes prediction more difficult.

Standard Scores

Before going on to the basic concept of correlation, let me spend a brief time talking about comparability of scores. In many situations where you are trying to predict success—for example, in the captain's position in a metropolitan police department—there is an attempt to predict that success by using a number of predictors, the most common being the written test, the oral boards, and perhaps some measure of time and grade.

If we have 100 candidates and we have the above three measures on all 100 candidates, we want to combine each of the three measures so that we can generate one final overall score for each candidate. Simply adding the three scores to one another can cause a number of problems. For example, let us assume that Sergeant Jones has been a sergeant for four years, he received an overall score of fifteen on the oral board, answered forty-five out of fifty questions correct on the written test. His overall score would be sixty-four. Sergeant Smith took the same test and received the following scores: $5 + 15 + 44 = 64$. Hopefully, one year's experience as a sergeant is worth more than one item on a written test when success in the captain's position is trying to be determined. What has happened here is that the police department, using this particular procedure, has tried to mix apples and oranges and it does not work.

Fortunately, there is a way to equate these scores in a simple calculation. It is known as standardization of scores or using standard scores. The procedure is uncomplicated and will be briefly described here. One rather ludicrous and unfair situation that can be demonstrated is what happens if the interviewer decides to use a scale of 1 to 1000 in his interview. This is unusual but any scale of measurement can be used. If someone decided to use a 1000 point scale in which the very outstanding candidates would be ranked closer to 1000 and the poorer candidates would be ranked closer to 1, adding simple raw scores of the three measures (oral board, written test, and experience) could lead to a very unfair picture.

This could easily result in the advantage a sergeant with ten years' experience has over a sergeant with one year's experience being wiped out by a mere whim of the interviewer (e.g. giving one sergeant a score of 690 and another sergeant a score of 600). When you have large scales, such as 1 to 1000, frequently interviewees who have been seen as essentially the same will be assigned different scores simply because of a variation of time or fatigue on the part of the interviewers, or because of some rather non–job-related qualities such as the candidate's hair was combed to a slightly better degree.

The standardization process is a simple one. The most common standardized score is the "Z" score. The formula for the Z score is simply to subtract the mean from the raw score and divide the remainder by the standard deviation of the distribution. Taking our array of scores from the sergeant's test, one would transfer the first raw score of 80 by subtracting the mean from it (80-72.1) and then dividing the remainder by the standard deviation which is 14.17. Thus the Z score for 80 is 0.56. Once you have performed this process with the raw scores in the distribution, they can be added to standardized scores of other distributions.

Take the example of the people who took the sergeant's test in the previous diagram (Figure 4), they have also taken an oral board and have a certain amount of experience behind them. It is not necessary to use these particular predictors in a promotional procedure, they are given simply as examples.) If we add the scores from Figure 8 across the three predictors (i.e. Don Andrews', score would equal 80 + 15 + 48) we are essentially adding apples and oranges. Our results are meaningless. If we want to combine the scores from one predictor with the scores of another predictor for the same person, we should standardize the distribution for each of the predictors. This can be done by using the Z transformation previously described, thereby standardizing each of the three predictor distributions.

When the raw scores are transformed into the Z scores, the latter distribution has a mean of zero and a standard deviation of one. Therefore, a person with a Z score of 1 is automatically located at one standard deviation above the mean. Similarly, a person with a Z score of −2 can automatically be located at a

Sergeant's Promotional Test

NAME	SCORES	ORAL BOARD	EXPERIENCE (Months in grade)
1. Andrews, Don	80	15	48
2. Atkins, Allen	76	12	54
3. Aubuchon, Kenneth	62	18	42
4. Austin, James	40	19.50	60
5. Binder, Richard	80	14	66
6. Birkemeier, John	84	10.75	48
7. Boesing, Jeanne	86	7	42
8. Bolen, Garry	91	13.45	69
9. Brady, Irene	84	11	42
10. Clark, Joseph	62	14	54
11. Clooney, Vincent	74	8.75	39
12. Coad, Daniel	80	10	45
13. Coleman, Clarence	78	15	51
14. Davis, Claude	60	11.25	42
15. Deering, Richard	92	17	69
16. Fairchild, Stephen	91	23	66
17. Fenwick, Shirley	80	16	60
18. Ferguson, Gerald	79	14	54
19. Foulks, Mike	62	12	79
20. Giardina, John	75	10.15	42
21. Gordon, Larry	58	16	60
22. Harper, David	49	18	73
23. Hart, George	54	22.25	78
24. Humphrey, Preston	52	17	66
25. Julius, Frank	62	14.50	54
26. King, Tim	67	12	48
27. Kirby, Edith	61	8.75	60
28. Lammer, Michael	88	18	66
29. Lato, Andrew	90	12	42
30. Martin, Terry	49	15	48
31. Miller, Joe	49	13	57
32. Mollet, Earl	57	14	60
33. Norton, David	89	17	73
34. O'Leary, Beth	71	16	66
35. Rosen, John	74	12.45	48
36. Schaefer, Roger	74	16.50	51
37. Smith, Larry	80	14.75	42
38. Taylor, Ronald	92	12.50	63
39. Thornton, Eva	87	11	36
40. Williams, John	65	16	54

Figure 8.

The Successful Police Officer

Sergeant's Promotional Test
Z Score

NAME	WRITTEN TEST SCORES	ORAL BOARD	EXPERIENCE (Months in Grade)	FINAL SCORE
1. Andrews, Don	.56	.23	—2.13	—1.34
2. Atkins, Allen	.27	—.64	—.41	—.78
3. Aubuchon, Kenneth	—.71	1.10	—3.84	—3.45
4. Austin, James	—2.26	1.53	1.31	.58
5. Binder, Richard	.56	—.06	3.03	3.53
6. Birkemeier, John	.84	—1.00	—2.13	—2.29
7. Boesing, Jeanne	.98	—2.09	—3.84	—4.95
8. Bolen, Garry	1.33	—.22	3.89	5.00
9. Brady, Irene	.84	—.93	—3.84	—3.93
10. Clark, Joseph	—.71	—.06	—.41	—1.18
11. Clooney, Vincent	.13	—1.58	—4.70	—6.15
12. Coad, Daniel	.56	—1.22	—2.98	—3.64
13. Coleman, Clarence	.42	.23	—1.26	—.61
14. Davis, Claude	—.85	—.86	—3.84	—5.55
15. Deering, Richard	1.40	.81	3.89	6.10
16. Fairchild, Stephen	1.33	2.55	3.03	6.91
17. Fenwick, Shirley	.56	.52	1.31	2.39
18. Ferguson, Gerald	.49	—.06	—.41	.02
19. Foulks, Mike	—.71	—.64	6.76	5.41
20. Giardina, John	.20	—1.18	—3.84	—4.82
21. Gordon, Larry	—.99	.52	1.31	.84
22. Harper, David	—1.63	1.10	5.04	4.51
23. Hart, George	—1.27	2.33	6.47	7.53
24. Humphrey, Preston	—1.42	.81	3.03	2.42
25. Julius, Frank	—.71	.08	—.41	—1.04
26. King, Tim	—.36	—.64	—2.13	—3.13
27. Kirby, Edith	—.78	—1.58	1.31	—1.05
28. Lammer, Michael	1.12	1.10	3.03	5.25
29. Lato, Andrew	1.26	—.64	—3.84	—3.22
30. Martin, Terry	—1.63	.23	—2.13	—3.53
31. Miller, Joe	—1.63	—.35	.45	—1.53
32. Mollet, Earl	—1.06	—.06	1.31	.19
33. Norton, David	1.19	.81	5.04	7.04
34. O'Leary, Beth	—.08	.52	3.03	3.47
35. Rosen, John	.13	—.51	—2.13	—2.51
36. Schaefer, Roger	.13	.66	—1.26	—.47
37. Smith, Larry	.56	.16	—3.84	—3.12
38. Taylor, Ronald	1.40	—.50	2.17	3.07
39. Thornton, Eva	1.05	—.93	—5.56	—5.44
40. Williams, John	—.50	.52	—.41	—.39

Figure 9.

point in that distribution of two standard deviations below the mean.

There are other standardized transformations including the T score which has a mean of 50 and a standard deviation of 10. This is primarily for situations where one would like to avoid working with negative numbers.

If we were to take the above set of distributions and transform them into T scores, the results would look like Figure 10. By combining the T scores in each distribution with one another, we would get the final overall predicted score for each person.

A logical question at this point that is frequently raised is does not such a process, although it makes data comparable from one predictor to the next, equally weight the three scores when, in fact, the management in the police department may want to emphasize the written test more than experience? The answer is yes, it does.

It is possible to weight the scores, such as 40 percent times the written test score (Z score) plus 40 percent times the oral board (Z score) plus 20 percent times the experience (Z score) equals overall predicted score.

This is a perfectly legitimate statistical procedure but should have some logic on which it is based. For example, if the job analysis that is done on the target position (the position for which the promotional list is being generated) reveals that 40 percent of the qualities necessary for the job can be measured by the written test and 40 percent by the oral board, then there is some justification for assigning these weights to those particular predictors. The percentages would be multiplied by each of the Z scores before they were added together to obtain the overall predicted score.

This is the exact spot where the importance of the standard deviation is readily seen. If the standard deviations for the three distributions are quite similar, there is no problem in assigning weights to different scores and coming out with the intended weightings. However, in some situations standard deviations are quite different from one distribution to another and this can present problems. The problems are not insurmountable, but one

The Successful Police Officer

Sergeant's Promotional Test
T Score

NAME	WRITTEN TEST SCORES	ORAL BOARD	EXPERIENCE (Months in Grade)	FINAL SCORE
1. Andrews, Don	55.57	52.29	28.74	136.60
2. Atkins, Allen	52.75	43.59	45.93	142.27
3. Aubuchon, Kenneth	42.87	60.98	11.55	115.40
4. Austin, James	27.35	65.33	63.12	155.80
5. Binder, Richard	55.57	49.39	80.31	185.27
6. Birkemeier, John	58.40	39.97	28.74	127.11
7. Boesing, Jeanne	59.81	29.10	11.55	100.46
8. Bolen, Garry	63.34	47.80	88.91	200.05
9. Brady, Irene	58.40	40.70	11.55	110.65
10. Clark, Joseph	42.87	49.39	45.93	138.19
11. Clooney, Vincent	51.34	34.17	2.95	88.46
12. Coad, Daniel	55.57	37.80	20.14	113.51
13. Coleman, Clarence	54.16	52.29	37.33	143.78
14. Davis, Claude	41.46	41.42	11.55	52.97
15. Deering, Richard	64.04	14.49	88.91	167.44
16. Fairchild, Stephen	63.34	75.48	80.31	219.13
17. Fenwick, Shirley	55.57	55.19	63.12	173.88
18. Ferguson, Gerald	54.87	49.39	45.93	150.19
19. Foulks, Mike	42.87	43.59	117.56	204.02
20. Giardina, John	52.04	38.23	11.55	101.82
21. Gordon, Larry	40.05	55.19	63.12	158.36
22. Harper, David	33.70	60.98	100.37	195.05
23. Hart, George	37.23	73.30	114.70	225.23
24. Humphrey, Preston	35.81	14.49	80.31	130.61
25. Julius, Frank	42.87	50.84	45.93	139.64
26. King, Tim	46.40	43.59	28.74	118.73
27. Kirby, Edith	42.17	34.17	63.12	139.46
28. Lammer, Michael	61.22	60.98	80.31	202.51
29. Lato, Andrew	62.63	43.59	11.55	117.77
30. Martin, Terry	33.70	52.29	28.74	114.73
31. Miller, Joe	33.70	46.49	54.53	134.72
32. Mollet, Earl	39.34	49.39	63.12	151.85
33. Norton, David	61.93	14.49	100.37	176.75
34. O'Leary, Beth	49.22	55.19	80.31	184.72
35. Rosen, John	51.34	44.90	28.74	124.98
36. Schaefer, Roger	51.34	56.64	37.33	145.31
37. Smith, Larry	55.57	51.56	11.55	118.68
38. Taylor, Ronald	64.04	45.04	71.97	181.05
39. Thornton, Eva	60.51	40.70	—5.64	95.57
40. Williams, John	44.99	55.19	45.93	146.11

Figure 10.

should be aware of them.

One problem can be easily demonstrated in a situation where ten candidates are being considered for a rank as captain in a department. Assume for a moment that all the candidates have had a minimum of three years in grade as sergeant and most of them have been on the force for quite a while and consequently most of them have an excess of ten years experience. It is not uncommon for some employers to take the position of giving credit for no more than ten years experience in grade. This is done to avoid giving an unfair advantage to the experienced candidate above and beyond what he deserves. Therefore, they will set a limit of about ten years, reasoning that the person who has that much experience in grade should be given credit for it but credit beyond that point is really not justified.

Consequently, we wind up in a situation with ten people all having the maximum allowable of ten years experience. To keep it simple, assume that the only other predictor is a written test. To further demonstrate the point, assume also that for some reason we wanted to give 80 percent weight to experience and only 20 percent weight to the written test. Even if we were to transform the scores into Z scores and then subsequently multiply the experience Z scores by 80 percent and the written test Z scores by 20 percent and then add them, the fact remains that 100 percent of the variance in the overall score is being contributed by written tests because there is no variance at all in the experience score (everyone has gotten ten years). Therefore, the weightings of 80 and 20 percent are "sham" ratings. *This is why it is so important to select predictors that generate variance.*

Even if some of the candidates had nine or even eight years experience with the majority having ten or more, the problem would still exist.

It is important in selecting predictors to make every effort possible in avoiding such a predicament. If one finds himself in this situation or in a similar situation where the scores do not vary, there are some statistical procedures such as normalizing the distribution that may work in some cases. There are some situations in which all types of statistical manipulations may not solve the problem. *Therefore, it is imperative to generate and develop predictors that provide variance in scores.*

The transformation of the forty raw scores of the sergeant's promotional test distribution are seen below. Each raw score is first transformed into a Z score and then into a T score. It is important to note that the absolute value of the score has not been changed even though the quantity is different. This transformation process is known as standardization or "transforming to a standardized distribution." This can be done to almost any array of scores and, as mentioned before, will allow comparison of scores from different distributions. For example, if you now say that Officer Green took the promotional examination and received a T score of 59 on the written test, and a T score of 50 on experience, and a T score of 41 on the oral board, you can immediately realize that he is almost one full standard deviation above the mean on the written, average on the experience, and almost one full standard deviation below the mean on the oral board.

Other important aspects of the standard deviation will be discussed later. One final concept to be mentioned before completing the statistical appendix is that of correlation.

Correlation

It is not uncommon for people to wonder about the relationship between two different variables (a variable is anything on which a group of people can vary, e.g. weight, height, number of brothers and sisters, amount of education, annual income). Up until now we have been talking about one distribution of scores. Let us now look at the relationship between two distributions of scores.

Is there a relationship between age and performance on the police captain promotional test? Is there a relationship between education and performance on the sergeant's promotional test? Do the younger sergeant candidates do better on the test than older candidates?

There can be an exact answer to these questions using a statistical procedure known as correlation. The process is not very complicated and there are one or two basic formulae into which one can plug scores and come up with a single number. That number reflects the degree of relationship between the two variables and is called a correlation coefficient. The correlation coefficient can vary from a minimum of -1.00 to a maximum of $+1.00$.

Let us look at a few examples. Suppose that we have ten sergeants within a particular division of a police department and we ask a captain who is familiar with all ten to rank their on-job performance by giving the most effective sergeant a rank of one, the second most effective the rank of two, and so on until he reaches the least effective which will have the rank of ten. Let us also assume that we have given these sergeants the paper and pencil promotional test that we plan to administer for sergeant in a few months. So now we can rank their performance on the paper and pencil test as well. Again we give the highest scoring person the rank of one, the next highest the rank of two, and the lowest scoring person the rank of ten. As a result, we can generate a table that looks like the one in Figure 11.

	Test Performance	*Job Performance*
Zeitsinger	1	2
Connors	2	1
Kavanaugh	3	4
Green	4	8
DuBois	5	3
Bray	6	5
Powers	7	7
Knowles	8	6
Pfeiffer	9	10
Gibbons	10	9

Figure 11.
A Ranking on Two Variables.

You can see by examining the table that there is a tendency for people who score high on the test such as Officers Zeitsinger, Connors, and Kavanaugh also to be ranked high on job performance. The same tendency is true down at the lower end of the scores for Officers Knowles, Pfeiffer, and Gibbons who were ranked low on job performance and also received low rankings on test performance. Where this trend or tendency for high ranking on one variable to be accompanied by high ranking on another variable is present, the correlation coefficient will get closer and closer to the value of +1.00. If the officers' job performance ranking had been identical to their test performance (i.e. Sergeant Zeitsinger would have been ranked one on job performance as well as on test performance and Officer Connors would have been ranked two, etc.) the correlation coefficient between the two variables would have been +1.00. This rarely happens because there are almost always exceptions and slight differences in rank. In addition, there are definite exceptions to the general rule, such as Officer Green who was ranked fourth from the top on test performance and yet was ranked eighth (two from the bottom) on job performance. The more exceptions like this there are, the lower the correlation would be. As a result, many correlation coefficients are between the values of 0.00 and 1.00 (e.g. 0.70, 0.32, 0.94, 0.17). The reader is encouraged to avoid the temptation to look at these correlations as percentages. *They are clearly not percentages.*

In the previous examples, the people who tend to score high on one variable also tend to score high on the other. This is called *positive* correlation. There is another possibility and that is that people who score high on one variable would tend to score low on the other variable as a general rule (see Figure 12).

The calculations yield a correlation coefficient of −0.75. What does this tell us? In addition to telling us that the relationship is negative (inverse), it also tells us that the relationship is a very strong one and that there is something besides just chance factors affecting the relationship of the two variables. However, it should be pointed out with as much emphasis as possible that the relationship between two variables does not necessarily imply that one variable *caused* the other. It should also be pointed out that a correlation of −0.75 is just as strong as the correlation of +0.75. They are simply in different directions.

Let us look at another correlation, this time between performance on the test and performance on the job. Do people who score

NAME	JOB	AGE	DIFFERENCE	D^2
Zeitsinger	2	10	-8	64
Connors	1	9	-8	64
Kavanaugh	4	7	-3	9
Green	8	8	0	0
DuBois	3	5	-2	4
Bray	5	6	-1	1
Powers	7	4	3	9
Knowles	6	3	3	9
Pfeiffer	10	1	9	81
Gibbons	9	2	7	49
			$\Sigma D^2 =$	290

$$RHO = 1 - \frac{6\Sigma D^2}{N(N^2-1)}$$

$$RHO = 1 - \frac{6(290)}{10(100-1)}$$

$$RHO = 1 - \frac{1740}{990}$$

$$RHO = 1 - 1.75$$

$$RHO = -0.75758$$

(e.g. Zeitsinger is the 2nd highest performing person and the youngest in age.)

Figure 12.

Correlation between age rank and job performance rank.

high on the written test (predictor) also actually do better on the job (see Figure 13)?

There are a number of ways of computing the correlation coefficient. If the test results come in ranked form, you can use the formula just used which is the rank-difference correlation (RHO). If the data comes in raw score form or Z score form, you can use a

NAME	TEST	JOB	DIFFERENCE	D^2
Zeitsinger	1	2	-1	1
Connors	2	1	1	1
Kavanaugh	3	4	-1	1
Green	4	8	-4	16
DuBois	5	3	2	4
Bray	6	5	1	1
Powers	7	7	0	0
Knowles	8	6	2	4
Pfeiffer	9	10	-1	1
Gibbons	10	9	1	1
			ΣD^2 = 30	

$$RHO = 1 - \frac{6\Sigma D^2}{N(N^2 - 1)}$$

$$RHO = 1 - \frac{6(30)}{10(100-1)}$$

$$RHO = 1 - \frac{180}{990}$$

$$RHO = 1 - 0.18$$

$$RHO = 0.81818$$

(e.g. Zeitsinger is the 2nd highest performing person and the youngest in age.)

Figure 13.
Correlation between test and job performance.

different measure of correlation coefficient which is called the Pearson product-moment correlation. The formula is the following:

$$r = \frac{N\Sigma XY - \Sigma X\Sigma Y}{\sqrt{[N\Sigma X^2 - (\Sigma X)^2][N\Sigma Y^2 - (\Sigma Y)^2]}}$$

(where r is the correlation coefficient)
N is the number of subjects

ΣXT is the sum of the cross products $\;(\text{i.e. } (X_1)\,(Y_1) + (X_2)\,(Y_2) + \ldots \ldots (X_n)\,(Y_n))$

$\Sigma X \Sigma Y$ is the sum of X's times the sum of Y's

ΣX^2 is the sum of the X^2's $\;(\text{i.e. } X_1^2 + X_2^2 + X_3^2 \ldots \ldots \ldots \ldots X_n^2)$

$(\Sigma X)^2$ is the square of ΣX

To see how this correlation would work, let us return to the array of data on the sergeant's promotional test raw scores. The product-moment correlation is also appropriate and useful when there are tied scores. Sometimes it is informative to see to what degree two predictors (test scores and scores on the oral board) correlated. Do people who score high on the test also score high on the oral board? Let us go through and use the product-moment correlation formula to correlate test scores and oral board scores (see Figure 14).

Before concepts of correlation, let us look at one more example of product-moment correlation. When one examines the relationship between two more predictors such as test scores and experience, they might be interested in the question, do people with more experience tend to get higher scores on the written test (see Figure 15)?

Pearson Product-Moment Correlation
of Test and Oral Board Scores

	TEST (X)	ORAL BOARD (Y)	X^2	Y^2	XY
1. Andrews, Don	80	15	6400	225	1200
2. Atkins, Allen	76	12	5776	144	912
3. Aubuchon, Kenneth	62	18	3844	324	1116
4. Austin, James	40	19.50	1600	380.25	780
5. Binder, Richard	80	14	6400	196	1120
6. Birkemeier, John	84	10.75	7056	115.56	903
7. Bodecker, Tim	86	7	7396	49	602
8. Bolen, Garry	91	13.45	8281	180.90	1223.95
9. Brady, Irene	84	11	7056	121	924
10. Clark, Joseph	62	14	3844	196	868
11. Clooney, Vincent	74	8.75	5476	76.56	647.50
12. Coad, Daniel	80	10	6400	100	800
13. Coleman, Clarence	78	15	6084	225	1170
14. Davis, Claude	60	11.25	3600	126.56	675
15. Deering, Richard	92	17	8464	289	1564
16. Fairchild, Stephen	91	23	8281	529	2093
17. Fenwick, Shirley	80	16	6400	256	1280
18. Ferguson, Gerald	79	14	6241	196	1106
19. Fischer, Stanley	62	12	3844	144	744
20. Giardina, John	75	10.15	5625	103.02	761.25
21. Gordon, Larry	58	16	3364	256	928
22. Harper, David	49	18	2401	324	882
23. Hart, George	54	22.25	2916	495.06	1201.50
24. Humphrey, Preston	52	17	2704	289	884
25. Julius, Frank	62	14.50	3844	210.25	899
26. Kipp, Fred	67	12	4489	144	804
27. Kirby, Edith	61	8.75	3721	76.56	533.75
28. Lammer, Michael	88	18	7744	324	1584
29. Lato, Andrew	90	12	8100	144	1080
30. Martin, Terry	49	15	2401	225	735
31. McPherson, Charles	49	13	2401	169	637
32. Mollet, Earl	57	14	3249	196	798
33. Norton, David	89	17	7921	289	1513
34. Richardson, Thomas	71	16	5041	256	1136
35. Rosen, John	74	12.45	5476	155	921.30
36. Schaefer, Roger	74	16.50	5476	272.25	1221
37. Smith, Larry	80	14.75	6400	217.56	1180
38. Taylor, Ronald	92	12.50	8464	156.25	1150
39. Thornton, Eva	87	11	7569	121	957
40. Weber, Jane	65	16	4225	256	1040

Figure 14a.

Appendix A

$SD_x = 14.36$ $\Sigma X = 2884$ $M_x = 72.1$
$SD_y = 3.84$ $\Sigma Y = 568.55$ $M_y = 14.21$
  $\Sigma X^2 = 215974$ $\Sigma XY = 40574.25$
  $\Sigma Y^2 = 8552.8025$
  $N = 40$

Formula for Pearson Product-Moment Correlation of Test and Oral Board Scores

$$r = \frac{N\Sigma XY - \Sigma X\Sigma Y}{\sqrt{[N\Sigma X^2 - (\Sigma X)^2]\ [N\Sigma Y^2 - (\Sigma Y)^2]}}$$

$$r = \frac{(40 \times 40574.25) - (2884 \times 568.55)}{\sqrt{[40(215974) - (2884)^2]\ [40(8552.78) - (568.55)^2]}}$$

$$r = \frac{1622970 - 1639698.2}{\sqrt{[8638960 - 8317456]\ [342111.2 - 323249.1]}}$$

$$r = \frac{-16728.2}{\sqrt{[321504]\ [18862.1]}}$$

$$r = \frac{-16728.2}{\sqrt{6064240598}} \quad \frac{-16728.2}{77873.23}$$

$r = -\ 0.2148$

Figure 14 a & b.

Pearson Product-Moment Correlation
Between Test and Experience

	TEST (X	EXPERIENCE (Y)	X^2	Y^2	XY
1. Andrews, Don	80	48	6400	2304	3840
2. Atkins, Allen	76	54	5776	2916	4104
3. Aubuchon, Kenneth	62	42	3844	1764	2604
4. Austin, James	40	60	1600	3600	2400
5. Binder, Richard	80	66	6400	4356	5280
6. Birkemeier, John	84	48	7056	2304	4032
7. Bodecker, Tim	86	42	7396	1764	3612
8. Bolen, Garry	91	69	8281	4761	6279
9. Brady, Irene	84	42	7056	1764	3528
10. Clark, Joseph	62	54	3844	2916	3348
11. Clooney, Vincent	74	39	5476	1521	2886
12. Coad, Daniel	80	45	6400	2025	3600
13. Coleman, Clarence	78	51	6084	2601	3978
14. Davis, Claude	60	42	3600	1764	2520
15. Deering, Richard	92	69	8464	4761	6348
16. Fairchild, Stephen	91	66	8281	4356	6006
17. Fenwick, Shirley	80	60	6400	3600	4800
18. Ferguson, Gerald	79	54	6241	2916	4266
19. Fischer, Stanley	62	79	3844	6241	4898
20. Giardina, John	75	42	5625	1764	3150
21. Gordon, Larry	58	60	3364	3600	3480
22. Harper, David	49	73	2401	5329	3577
23. Hart, George	54	78	2916	6084	4212
24. Humphrey, Preston	52	66	2704	4356	3432
25. Julius, Frank	62	54	3844	2916	3348
26. Kipp, Fred	67	48	4489	2304	3216
27. Kirby, Edith	61	60	3721	3600	3660
28. Lammer, Michael	88	66	7744	4356	5808
29. Lato, Andrew	90	42	8100	1764	3780
30. Martin, Terry	49	48	2401	2304	2352
31. McPherson, Charles	49	57	2401	3249	2793
32. Mollet, Earl	57	60	3249	3600	3420
33. Norton, David	89	73	7921	5329	6497
34. Richardson, Thomas	71	66	5041	4356	4686
35. Rosen, John	74	48	5476	2304	3552
36. Schaefer, Roger	74	51	5476	2601	3774
37. Smith, Larry	80	42	6400	1764	3360
38. Taylor, Ronald	92	63	8464	3969	5796
39. Thornton, Eva	87	36	7569	1296	3132
40. Weber, Jane	65	54	4225	2916	3510

Figure 15a.

Appendix A

$SD_x = 14.36$	$\Sigma X = 2884$	$M_x = 72.1$
$SD_y = 11.455$	$\Sigma Y = 2217$	$M_y = 55.425$
	$\Sigma X^2 = 215974$	$\Sigma XY = 158864$
	$\Sigma Y^2 = 127995$	
	$N = 40$	

Formula for correlation between test and experience

$$r = \frac{N\Sigma XY - \Sigma X \Sigma Y}{\sqrt{\left[N\Sigma X^2 - (\Sigma X)^2\right]\left[N\Sigma Y^2 - (\Sigma Y)^2\right]}}$$

$$r = \frac{(40 \times 158864) - (2884 \times 2217)}{\sqrt{\left[40(215974) - (2884)^2\right]\left[40(127995) - (2217)^2\right]}}$$

$$r = \frac{6354560 - 6393828}{\sqrt{\left[8638960 - 8317456\right]\left[5119800 - 4915089\right]}}$$

$$r = \frac{-39268}{\sqrt{\left[321504\right]\left[204711\right]}}$$

$$r = \frac{-39268}{\sqrt{658154053410}} \quad \frac{-39268}{256545.13}$$

$$r = -0.1531$$

Figure 15 a & b

Appendix B

ITEM ANALYSIS
(Test Construction)

THIS APPENDIX is written for those people who are confronted with the task of either writing a paper and pencil test for a specific position or correcting and improving upon an existing paper and pencil test. Both situations frequently occur and there are a number of things that can be done to improve on the past paper and pencil test by rebuilding it or simply creating a new one.

However, it should be stated at the outset that the paper and pencil test, while having the advantage of objectivity insofar as it can be scored by independent scorers and the same score generated, is a very restrictive method of gathering job-related information. For example, it is quite difficult to generate sound paper and pencil questions which will effectively measure supervisory skills and potential. In many positions, these skills are very important. The paper and pencil test is most effective in measuring knowledges of certain specific job areas.

Why is it used so often? The answer to this question is primarily because of its objectivity and because of its utility. This refers to its ability to be administered to large groups of people in a very standardized and quick manner.

Item Writing

Each question is referred to as an item, in the paper and pencil test it typically takes the form of multiple choice, fill-in, or true/false. The true/false format is simply a revised version of the multiple-choice approach involving two alternatives rather than four or five. However, the "provide an answer" approach is distinctly different and usually involves filling in a blank. This approach calls for a slightly different process on the part of the test taker, namely, that of recall rather than the process of recognition which is called for in the multiple-choice approach.

The advantage of recall or "provide an answer" as a method is, according to its supporters, that it is more like the real-life situation which requires the job incumbent to recall the appropriate answer rather than recognize it. The disadvantage is a slight drop in objectivity particularly when you come to borderline answers. For example, if the correct answer is "the President's Commission on Law Enforcement Report, 1974" and the given answer is "The Law Enforcement Commission's Report, 1974" do you give credit, if so do you give total credit, and if not, what partial credit is allowed. These kinds of questions call for judgments all of which are difficult to anticipate and all of which may lead to a type of difference in judgments which ultimately may result in some drop in objectivity.

On the other hand, the proponents of the multiple-choice item contend that frequently the multiple-choice format which requires recognition is more job related because on the job, behavior usually involves a series of alternatives for the person to choose from. In addition, it is more easily objectified.

The multiple-choice question should be phrased in as simple terms as possible to identify the given area of knowledge. It can even follow the basic test plan which lists all of the basic knowledge areas to be covered in the test and the importance assigned to those knowledge areas and finally the number of items in the test to be administered. Such a plan could involve a logic as follows: The job analysis noted that knowledge of local city ordinances was considered essentially twice as important as knowledge of car maintenance, therefore, twice as many items on the topic of ordinances should be included as on the topic of car maintenance. There are no hard and fast rules here but some systematic organization of test items is far better than simply reviewing material and putting the items where one finds them.

Once you have developed a general test plan, you can examine the overall length of your test and it is recommended that multiple-choice tests exceed seventy-five items in order to achieve a respectable level of reliability (see Appendix A). Generally, the shorter the test the lower the reliability. Sound test reliabilities typically range from a low of 0.75 up to 0.95. A general rule is that the more items you can have the more reliable the test would be. Obviously you reach your saturation point somewhere around 125 to 150 items after which additional items do not mean that much in terms of greater reliability. You are encouraged to recognize that these are general rules and there are exceptions in given situations.

When you write an item you should have a clear concept of what you are trying to measure, and describe the question or item in as clear and concise a manner as possible. The stem should be as brief as clarity will permit and the alternatives should reflect clarity as well as common ideas associated with the particular question. The alternatives should have a correct answer which is clearly stated and upon which experts have agreed. The alternatives are also referred to as distractors and should do just that. If a distractor is so outlandish and far off the mark that no one chooses it, then it is not really a distractor. Consequently it is not doing its job.

Distractors should reflect commonly held misbeliefs and frequently chosen misconceptions about the question. Distractors have to fill that difficult position of being plausible alternatives without being hairsplitting alternatives.

The question stem should not omit a basic assumption that the test writer is making. All conditions and assumptions that render the test questions as self-explanatory should be included.

Actually, item writing can be broken down into two phases. The first phase has already been discussed and includes the development of concise and clear questions with reasonable and effective distractors and clear distinct answers. Phase two involves the evaluation of both the tests and each specific item in the test along a number of lines.

The first element in an item analysis to be discussed here is "the difficulty index." Typically, a statistical analysis of the results of the test is called an item analysis and examines the overall test as well as each individual item. The difficulty index is simply a percentage of the population taking the test (norm group) who accurately answered the question. For example, a test item having a difficulty index of 0.95 indicates that 95 percent of the population accurately answered the question. Concurrently, an item having a difficulty index of 20 percent indicates that 20 percent of the population got the item right but 80 percent answered it incorrectly. While there is no ultimate ideal in this area, it is reasonable to hope for an equal distribution of highly difficult items, moderately difficult items, and very easy items.

A corollary indicator or item measurement is the percentage of the population choosing each of the alternative responses to the correct one, as the following demonstrates:

1. The first president of the United States was . . .
   a. Abraham Lincoln   Percentage answering: 20%
   b. Jimmy Carter   2%
   c. George Washington   75%
   d. John Adams   3%

As the above item indicates, the correct answer has item difficulty of 75 percent and alternative *a* does appear to be a reasonable distractor insofar as 20 percent of those answering the question chose that alternative. The other two distractors need some work and should be modified to increase their distractive power. This is the kind of information that can be generated by item analysis to assist the item writer in improving his test for the next administration.

An overall test indicator is given as part of a typical item analysis and this is the reliability coefficient. Typically, one would want this to be in the 80s and 90s but could accept it if it were in the 70s. When you get substantially below 0.70 then you should consider increasing the number of items in your test.

On a given item, its ability to discriminate is usually a correlation coefficient between a given item and the overall test. A high correlation, such as the people who do well on the item also do well on the test, is a positive indicator for a given item.

There are many different computer item analysis programs and one should shop around until they find specifically what they want. It is also possible to have a program tailor-made for your own purposes.   Whichever format you use, it is useful to systematically review test items after administration to make sure that they do not have items that are weak or have no distracting power within them. A test which may, on the surface, look valid (face-valid) could actually be a poor test.

Setting a time limit for a test is always a difficult chore and there are no exact guidelines to be used here. However, the test developer is urged to field test the instrument (test) and get some feel for how long it takes a person working straight through without stopping to complete it. If the job is not one which involves a great deal of time pressure and speed is not critical, then a harsh time limit should not be established.

Developing and administering tests and readministering them without item analysis is like a pilot flying without instruments, he has a hunch of where he is but he is not sure.

One of the uses of item analysis is to cluster together items that measure the same thing (KSA) and determine the reliability of that particular cluster, and if it is a significant enough K,S, or A to require a separate subtest.

Appendix C

ADDITIONAL FAIR EMPLOYMENT ISSUES

THE WHOLE issue of fair employment as it bears on the process of selection can become a complicated one with people who cite this court case or that decision. The literature abounds with articles of a practical nature as well as some rather philosophical papers about the goodness or badness of fair employment legislation.

The objective of this appendix is not to tie up these problems in a neat little package but to look at the phenomenon of selection from both a practical as well as an ethical perspective. This society will rise together or fall together and a major factor determining which it will be is the provision of equal employment opportunity made available to people on the basis of ability rather than such variables as race, sex, or national origin.

To appreciate the fair amount of adverse impact, one should think of the selection process as a pipeline with a series of filters. If a given filter screens out people on the basis of ability then the percentages of protected and unprotected classes being admitted should be roughly the same. However, if the rate of selection for a protected class drops below 80 percent of the rate of selection for an unprotected class, the federal legislation, more particularly the FEA guidelines, define that as adverse impact. Therefore, it would be useful for a law enforcement agency to examine its selection system to identify whether such adverse impact exists and to see if the percentages of protected classes applying for positions in their organization roughly represents the percentage of protected classes in the surrounding geographical area (as represented in the standard metropolitan statistical area—SMSA).

There are many alternative ways of defining adverse impact, however, there appear to be two basic solutions to the problem of unequal employment opportunity. The first solution I will label "job-related selection systems." This approach admits that there has been discrimination in the past and that it is an evil to be remedied. The remedy to be applied is sound analysis of specific jobs and the development of job-related selection systems for each position, including a critical evaluation of different selection components including recruitment to make sure that protected classes are encouraged to approach and progress through the selection system. This approach contends that any other solution would involve reverse discrimination and simply add one evil on top of the second thereby creating more problems than it solved.

The second solution is labeled "catch-up." Like the first solution, the second recognizes that the lack of equal opportunity has been and continues to be an evil in this society that needs to be remedied. However, this solution calls for sound job analyses and job-related selection systems but goes on to insist that the first solution is inadequate because it would essentially result in an extremely slow process whereby protected classes will take generations to just get into a position where they would be considered for a promotion. This is particularly true if you are talking about any substantial number of minorities or other protected class members reaching high positions within the next ten years.

Frankly, I see a great deal of logic in both arguments even though I have a natural aversion for anything that smacks of quotas. In addition to undercutting the merit principles on which selection systems are based, quotas have other insidious impacts. They call into question the legitimacy of a person getting a position because of membership in a protected class. If large groups of people are put into a position primarily based on class membership rather than sound broad measures of ability to do the job, there is a built-in disaster for the upward mobility of that group. The disaster is the inevitable adverse impact which will occur when the protected classes who are put in without regard to a performance score on a test, or with a very low score on such a predictor, do much worse than people who were screened on some kind of selection instrument such as a knowledge test. When the promotion exam comes up, the unprotected class is going to perform at a much higher level than the protected class and the inevitable adverse impact is upon us.

Anyone who has worked in this field knows that there are no perfect or even near perfect solutions. However, I would offer the following alternative for consideration. *If there are going to have to be quotas,* then both groups (protected and unprotected classes) should be screened on some type of rough selection instrument and then put into the job only after an equal number has been placed in some kind of job simulation procedure. Such procedures could involve a system such as the assessment center. These job simulation methods are less discriminatory and in some cases nondiscriminatory. In addition, they are more job related and an eligible list based on this type of selection device would produce candidates who have more skills for the job than a simple paper and pencil screener which generates a list from which even very low scores have to be chosen.

The ratios of protected and unprotected classes could be worked out but could even be a 50–50 ratio with the understanding that people would be put into the job based on the level of performance generated in the job simulation program. Minorities and other protected class members could be used as part of the judges involved in the job simulation procedure, thereby giving that group a feeling of involvement as well as a real involvement in the whole selection process.

Appendix D

SIGNIFICANCE TABLE

Significance of Pearson's r

$n-2$	.10	.05	.02	.01	.001
1	.98769	.99692	.999507	.999877	.9999988
2	.90000	.95000	.98000	.990000	.99900
3	.8054	.8783	.93433	.95873	.99116
4	.7293	.8114	.8822	.91720	.97406
5	.6694	.7545	.8329	.8745	.95074
6	.6215	.7067	.7887	.8343	.92493
7	.5822	.6664	.7498	.7977	.8982
8	.5494	.6319	.7155	.7646	.8721
9	.5214	.6021	.6851	.7348	.8471
10	.4973	.5760	.6851	.7079	.8233
11	.4762	.5529	.6339	.6835	.8010
12	.4575	.5324	.6120	.6614	.7800
13	.4409	.5139	.5923	.6411	.7603
14	.4259	.4973	.5742	.6226	.7420
15	.4124	.4821	.5577	.6055	.7246
16	.4000	.4683	.5425	.5897	.7084
17	.3887	.4555	.5285	.5751	.6932
18	.3783	.4438	.5155	.5614	.6787
19	.3687	.4329	.5034	.5487	.6652
20	.3598	.4227	.4921	.5368	.6524
25	.3233	.3809	.4451	.4689	.5974
30	.2960	.3494	.4093	.4487	.5541
35	.2746	.3246	.3810	.4182	.5189
40	.2573	.3044	.3578	.3932	.4896
45	.2428	.2875	.3384	.3721	.4648
50	.2306	.2732	.3218	.3541	.4433
60	.2108	.2500	.2948	.3248	.4078
70	.1954	.2319	.2737	.3017	.3799
80	.1829	.2172	.2565	.2830	.3568
90	.1726	.2050	.2422	.2673	.3375
100	.1638	.1946	.2301	.2540	.3211

Appendix E

SAMPLE IN-BASKET

T HE FOLLOWING IN-BASKET items constitute a portion of the in-basket used for the assessment center in developing a promotional list for the position of captain within the Kansas City, Missouri, Police Department and is reproduced here with the permission of the Kansas City Police Department.

Police Captain In-Basket
(Assistant Division Commander)

For the next three hours you are going to play the role of an Assistant Division Commander with the Kansas City, Missouri, Police Department.

The following information describes your situation:

Your name is Bruce Wayne. You have been employed by the Kansas City Police Department since January, 1977. You and your family returned home from a two-week vacation Monday afternoon, *September 1, 1977*, at 2100 hours. Major Alvin Davis, Commander, *West Patrol Division,* telephoned to tell you that you were promoted to Captain and assigned to his division, effective August 25, 1977. You will command the *III watch.*

Major Davis informs you that he is aware that you are leaving on a two-week military leave at *0500 hours on Tuesday, September 2, 1977.* Prior to his retirement, your predecessor, Captain Arlie Gonn, had been on sick leave and there are several items in your in-basket that require your attention. The station clerk will package your in-basket and have it delivered to the security office at the airport. You can pick it up and handle the items during the three hour flight to San Francisco. Sergeant White, of this department, is returning from a visit to San Francisco and will meet your plane and return with your material.

It is now 0500 hours, Tuesday, September 2, 1977. You must work alone and have access only to the materials found in your in-basket. It is important that you indicate in writing what you plan to do with each item in your package so action can be taken while you are in San Francisco. You should write memos, reports, and make notes to yourself, or to any other personnel in your department. You should also

143

plan any phone calls you intend to make when you return. *Every action you take or plan to take should be in writing.* Clip any notes, memos, or reports to the item(s) they refer to.

Remember you are Captain Bruce Wayne. The time is 0500 hours, Tuesday, September 2, 1977. *You will not return to your assignment until 1600 hours, September 17, 1977.*

Item Index
Captain's In-Basket Exercise

1. Organizational Chart — West Patrol Division
2. Assignment Roster — III Watch — West Patrol Division
3. Calendar — September, 1977
4. Calendar — October, 1977
5. Memo — Mrs. Rightous called, remind Capt. Gonn before 9–5–77
6. Memo — All City Charity Fund Drive
7. Evaluation of warrant by beat program
8. Memo — Visitation of Spanish police official
9. Memo from Sgt. Stronger re: P.O. Sharon Marks
9A. Memo from P.O. Sharon Marks re: desk assignment
10. Memo from Sgt. Harris re: Sgt. Brown
11. Route slip re: Mrs. Crump
11A. Letter from Mrs. Crump — juvenile activity
12. Memo — identification of training needs
13. Memo from Sgt. Hack — assignment of relief officers
14. Memo from Sgt. Olden re: P.O. Prettyman
15. Bulletin — Deceased officer — Capt. Gonn
16. Memo from Capt. Swoon — vice activity
17. Sealed letter
18. Internal Affairs investigation
19. Memo from Capt. Snyder — rock concert
20. Letter from Dr. Freud re: Sgt. Brown
21. Interdepartment mail from "Ray" recruit assignments
22. Letter from Realty Company re: protection of vacant houses
23. Note from Ray Rogges to Capt. Gonn

WEST PATROL DIVISION

September, 1977

Major Alvin Davis
Commander

P.O. Fred Brooks
Aide

I Watch	II Watch	III Watch
Captain John Jellis	Captain Roy Rogges	Captain Bruce Wayne
Assistant Division Commander	Assistant Division Commander	Assistant Division Commander

WEST PATROL DIVISION
Assignment Roster
Watch III
Desk Sergeant — Sgt. Lee Hack
Station Clerk — Civ. Ann Give
Desk Officer — P.O. Joe Miller

Section 110		*Section 130*	
Sgt. Edward Brown	R-110	Sgt. Paul Olden	R-130
P.O. Joseph Blue	R-111	P.O. Charles Young	R-131
P.O. William Johnson	R-112	P.O. Leslie Prettyman	R-132
P.O. John Smith	R-113	P.O. Jessie Terryberry	R-133
P.O. William Cruz	R-114	P.O. JoAnn Downey	R-133
P O. Janet Clark	R-115	P.O. Heck Zee	R-134
P.O. Greg Wilson	R-115	P.O. Willie Shoemaker	R-135
P.O. James Rogers	R-119	P.O. Brent Zaggis	R-139
Section 120		*Section 140*	
Sgt. Joseph Lookun	R-120	Sgt. Mark Stronger	R-140
P.O. Arnold Blow	R-121	P O. Sharon Marks	R-141
P.O. Bill Rich	R-122	P.O. Fred Grope	R-141
P.O. Ronald Tensive	R-123	P.O. Walter Stitch	R-142
P.O. Susan Smitty	R-124	P.O. William Winder	R-143
P.O. Robert Lynn	R-124	P.O. Robert Uprite	R-144
P.O. Will Pennies	R-125	P.O. Jansen Rollo	R-145
P.O. Dan Suggin	R-129	P.O. Homer Gumby	R-149

Relief Officers

Sgt. Dan Monday	P.O. Chris Levi	P.O. Vicky Polen
Sgt. Bill Marris	P.O. Zack Browning	P.O. Norman Mann
P.O. James Allwrong	P.O. Lowell Wolfe	P.O. Lester Snodgrass
P.O. Charles Left	P.O. Arthur Frams	P.O. Melvin Shorts
P.O. Carl Johnson	P.O. Joe Sanchez	P.O. Jimmy Running

Evidence Technicians

P.O. Gerald Glance
P.O. Teddy Wright

SEPTEMBER 1977

S	M	T	W	T	F	S
				1	2	3
4	5	6	7 Task force presentation 1300hrs. 8	9	10	11
12	13	14	15 Chieff staff meeting 16	17	18	19
20	21	22	23	24	25	26
27	28	29	30			

Mayor - council tour
Handouts/display

2000hrs. Mr. Rogthour

Evaluations
Hank olsen

OCTOBER 1977

S	M	T	W	T	F	S
			1	2	3	4
5	6	7	8	9	10	11
12	13	14	15	16	17	18
19 *chiefs' staff meeting* 20		21	22	23	24	25
26	27	28	29	30	31	

Things to Do Today

1. Capt: Gonn
2. Mr. Rightous called again —
3. said she would not be
4. responsibile for the actions
5. of her group if you did not
6. miet with them!
7.
8. Ann G.
9. 8-27-77
10.

APPOINTMENTS Amos Ann —

1.
2. Remind me of This before
3. Sept. 5 TH
4. Capt Gonn
5.

DEPARTMENT OF POLICE
KANSAS CITY, MISSOURI

INTERDEPARTMENT COMMUNICATION

To **All Commanding Officers**

Subject **Department Participation — All City Charity Fund Drive**

All City Charity Fund Drive
Percent Participation By Bureau

BUREAU	% Participating 1975	% Participating 1976	% Participating 1977
Administration	85.2	88.6	91.4
Service	90.2	92.1	91.0
Investigations	85.0	85.7	83.9
PATROL			
Central Division	93.8	94.1	93.9
South Division	78.6	87.2	90.4
Northeast Division	87.3	89.6	92.3
West Division	88.5	84.3	72.4

Major Davis

(Dept.)_____ (SIGNED) _Lt. a// Hallow_

Date _8-14-7 7_ _____ Approved _____

Form 191 P.D.   COMMANDING

ROUTING SLIP

_____ 8 - 27 _____ 19 77

Memo To:

Chief _____ Sgt. _____

Lt. Col. __*Davis*_____ Det. _____

Major _____ Off. _____

Capt. _____

☐ Read and Return   ☐ For Approval   ☐ Contact Me
☐ Read and Forward   ☐ Officer's File   ☐ For Comments
☐ For Signature   ☐ Report From Officer   ☐ Please Handle
☐ Reply, My Signature   ☐ Investigate & Return   ☐ Advise Disposition
☐ Reply, Your Signature   ☐ Your Information   ☐ By:_____ 19_____
☐ Officer Sign & Return   ☑ Recommendation   ☐ _____

Remarks: _Al – Have your people look this over and let me know their recommendations by 9-10 will have a meeting the 12TH to dis'Caran_

Lt. Col. Westfall

☐ Over   Office: _OPa . Bureau_

Form 134 (Rev. 12-71)

ROUTING SLIP

_8 - 29_ 19 _77_

Memo To:

Chief _____ Sgt. _____

Lt. Col. _____ Det. _____

Major _____ Off. _____

Capt. _Wayne_____

☐ Read and Return   ☐ For Approval   ☐ Contact Me

☐ Read and Forward   ☐ Officer's File   ☐ For Comments

☐ For Signature   ☐ Report From Officer   ☐ Please Handle

☐ Reply, My Signature   ☐ Investigate & Return   ☐ Advise Disposition

☐ Reply, Your Signature   ☐ Your Information   ☐ By:_____19_____

☐ Officer Sign & Return   ☑ Recommendation   ☐ _____

Remarks: _Look this over and let me know your recommendations by 9-8-77. Lt Col. Westfall wants to discuss this with all the Div. Co's on the 12TH_

By: _Maj Davis_

Office: _West Div. Commander_

☐ Over

Form 134 (Rev. 12-71)

MEMORANDUM

August 22, 1977

TO: Major Richard Hatfield, Commanding, Administrative
       Analysis Div.

FROM: Captain Edward Price, Commanding, Staff Inspection
        Unit

SUBJECT: Synopsis: Evaluation of Warrant List by Beat Pro-
                     gram

Sir:

An evaluation of the Warrant List by Beat Program was conducted, pursuant to a directive by the Assistant Chief of Police,
to determine if the program, which was discontinued February
12, 1976 and reimplemented July, 1976, had had any effect upon
the number of warrants being disposed of. The evaluation had
the further purpose of determining compliance with the provi-
sions of General Order 75-05, Warrant List by Beat Program.

The returned warrant lists for three program cycles were au-
dited and interviews were conducted with various effected department members.

It was found that there was no noticeable positive effect in
the number of warrants disposed of after reimplementation of the
program. With the exception of the South Central Patrol Sectors,
less than half of the patrol beat officers are returning the warrant
lists, as required by the general order. Some warrant lists appear
not to have been worked at all. On the average, fewer than 10
percent of the names listed as having outstanding warrants were
subject to attempts by officers to make contact. It was projected
from the audit of the returned warrant list that approximately 38
percent of the persons listed on the beat printouts would not be
contactable, because they had changed residences, had given false
addresses, or because a programming conflict had caused printing
addresses on the wrong beat printout. The audit and the interviews conducted indicated that patrol personnel assign a low prior-
ity to working the warrant lists. There are no quantitative standards or objectives established department-wide relative to the service of warrants listed on the Warrant Lists by Beat. On the posi-

tive side, a commendable effort had been made at the South Central Patrol Station to facilitate compliance with General Order 75–05.

Based upon the assumption that it is desirable for the Department to have a program of attempting to serve backlogged warrants and on the opinion that it is better to have no program than to have one that isn't working, it was recommended that the current general order be augmented by orders issued by the Operations Bureau Commander strengthening the program with objectives and priorities agreed upon by his subordinate commanders. It was further recommended that the methods for maintaining accountability for the warrants lists at the South Central Station be adopted at all stations at a cost of about $170.00 and that Sgt. Thomas Ewing and Major Clark Kint be commended for development of the method.

With a view to the future, it was suggested that the possibility of making the issuance of city licenses and permits contingent upon satisfaction of outstanding city warrants be pursued, particularly after the Clerk of the Court assumes responsibility for filing all city warrants later this year.

Illustrations are attached to this report which summarize the findings of the evaluation of the Warrant List by Beat Program.

Captain Edward Price
Commanding Staff Inspection Unit

CEP:jr

LIST OF COMMON DIMENSIONS

Career ambition — Motivation to advance to higher job levels; active efforts toward self-development.

Creativity — Ability to come up with imaginative solutions in business situations, and to recognize and accept imaginative solutions and innovations.

Decisiveness — Readiness to make decisions or to render judgments.

Energy — Ability to achieve a high activity level.

Flexibility — Ability to modify behavioral style and management approach to reach a goal.

Impact — Ability to create a good first impression, to command attention and respect, to show an air of confidence, and to achieve personal recognition.

Independence — Taking action based on own convictions rather than through a desire to please others.

Initiative — Actively influencing events rather than passively accepting; self-starting.

Judgment — Ability to reach logical conclusions based on the evidence at hand.

Leadership — Effectiveness in getting ideas accepted and in guiding a group or an individual to accomplish a task.

Listening skill — Ability to pick out important information in oral communications.

Management control — Appreciation of need for control and maintenance of control over processes, subordinates, and tasks.

Motivation — Importance of work in personal satisfaction, and the desire to achieve at work.

Oral communication skill — Effectiveness of expression in individual or group situations (includes gestures and nonverbal communications).

Planning and organizing — Effectiveness in planning and organizing own activities and those of a group.

Problem analysis — Effectiveness in seeking out pertinent data and in determining the source of the problem.

Range of interests — Breadth and diversity of interests, concern for personal and organizational environment, and a desire to participate actively in events.

Risk-taking — Ability to take calculated risks based on sound judgment.

Sensitivity — Skill in perceiving and reacting sensitively to the needs of others. Objectivity in perceiving impact of self on others.

Stress tolerance — Stability of performance under pressure and opposition.

Tenacity — Tendency to stay with a problem or line of thought until the matter is settled.

Use of delegation — Ability to use subordinates effectively and to understand where a decision can best be made.

Work standards — Desire to do a good job for its own sake.

Written communication skill — Ability to express ideas clearly in writing in good grammatical form.

Appendix G

SAMPLE SELECTION SYSTEM PLAN
FOR ENTRY-LEVEL POLICE OFFICER

Knowledges, Skills, Abilities, or Personal Characteristics	Application Review	Screening Interview	Written Test	Oral Board	Medical	Psychiatric	Working Test Period	Un-measurable
Ability to drive an automobile.	X							
Reading ability.			X					
Physical qualifications:								
a. Vision					X			
b. Cardiac					X			
c. Other					X			
Ability to understand simple verbal directions.			X					
Verbal communication skills.				X			X	
Ability to effectively interact with fellow officers.						X	X	
Ability to effectively interact with citizens, etc.				X		X	X	

Appendix H

SAMPLE INTERVIEWER FORM

A Sample Oral Board Rating Form

Position _____ Date _____

Candidate's Name _____

Instructions

The results of an oral board are no better than the preparation, job knowledge, and honest effort that go into them. In fairness to all candidates, each interviewer should:
1. Have a clear understanding of
   a) the position being filled and the specific qualities he is being asked to measure in the interview, and
   b) the rating scales and how to complete the form.
2. Rate each job quality independently of the others.
3. Be familiar with sound interviewing techniques.
4. Record ratings independently of the other raters.

I. PROBLEM ANALYSIS: The ability to gather information necessary for a logical decision.
(Circle one number.)
   1. Low—very little of the quality was demonstrated
   2. Below average—a slight degree of the quality was demonstrated
   3. Average—a moderate degree of the quality was shown
   4. Above average—a substantial amount of the quality was shown
   5. Excellent—an outstanding amount of the quality was shown.

II. JUDGMENT: The ability to arrive at logical conclusions.
   1. Low—very little of the quality was demonstrated
   2. Below average—a slight degree of the quality was demonstrated

3. Average—a moderate degree of the quality was shown
4. Above average—a substantial amount of the quality was shown
5. Excellent—an outstanding amount of the quality was shown

III. PLANNING SKILLS: The ability to plan and organize one's efforts and those of others in an efficient way.
1. Low—very little of the quality was demonstrated
2. Below average—a slight degree of the quality was demonstrated
3. Average—a moderate degree of the quality was shown
4. Above average—a substantial amount of the quality was shown
5. Excellent—an outstanding amount of the quality was shown

IV. DELEGATION: The ability to recognize where in an organization a decision should be made and direct that decision accordingly.
1. Low—very little of the quality was demonstrated
2. Below average—a slight degree of the quality was demonstrated
3. Average—a moderate degree of the quality was shown
4. Above average—a substantial amount of the quality was shown
5. Excellent—an outstanding amount of the quality was shown

V. SUPERVISORY FIRMNESS: The ability to forcefully represent management's viewpoints to subordinates when this is called for.
1. Low—very little of the quality was demonstrated
2. Below average—a slight degree of the quality was demonstrated
3. Average—a moderate degree of the quality was shown
4. Above average—a substantial amount of the quality was shown

5. Excellent—an outstanding amount of the quality was shown

(Additional Qualities)

VI. _____

_____

1. Low—very little of the quality was demonstrated
2. Below average—a slight degree of the quality was demonstrated
3. Average—a moderate degree of the quality was shown
4. Above average—a substantial amount of the quality was shown
5. Excellent—an outstanding amount of the quality was shown

VII. _____

_____

1. Low—very little of the quality was demonstrated
2. Below average—a slight degree of the quality was demonstrated
3. Average—a moderate degree of the quality was shown
4. Above average—a substantial amount of the quality was shown
5. Excellent—an outstanding amount of the quality was shown

Appendix I

SAMPLE SELECTION SYSTEM AUDIT

	TOTAL	White	%w	Black	%b
1. Applied	253	184		69	
2. Completed application form	213	163	88%	50	72%
3. Residence*	194	150	92%	44	88%
4. School absences	165	132	88%	33	75%
5. Transcript scores	100	85	64%	15	45%
6. Showed for testing	94	81	95%	13	86%
7. Passed test program	69	62	76%	7	53%
8. Showed for interview	68	61	98%	7	100%
9. Passed interview	47	41	67%	6	85%

*This employer served a specific residential area.

Appendix J

GLOSSARY

Adverse effect/impact — Differential rate of selection (for hire, promotion, etc.) which works to the disadvantage of an applicant subgroup, especially protected classes.

Applicant population — The group of individuals within a geographical area with identifiable characteristics from which applicants for employment are obtained.

Affirmative action — An activity initiated by an employer which contributes toward the greater utilization of minorities, females, the elderly, and the disabled.

Affirmative action plan — Document required by the government under regulations of the Office of Federal Contracts Compliance Programs. The employer is obliged to compare the internal distribution of minorities and females to their incidence in the external labor market and to determine whether or not he is at parity with the external labor market.

Aptitude — The extent to which a person may be expected to succeed in acquiring new skills or knowledge in a particular area.

Average — Same as measure of central tendency. In the more popular vocabulary, it is used the same as the mean or arithmetic mean.

BFOQ or BOQ — Stands for the bona fide occupational qualification which is the minimum qualification requirement that is needed to be hired and succeed on the job.

Bimodal distribution — Distribution of scores which has two distinct scores which are the most frequently occurring.

Biserial correlation coefficient — A measure of the relation between two variables, one of which falls into many classes or categories and one of which falls into just two categories. The latter variable is assumed to be continuous and normally distributed, although it is expressed in only two classes.

Ceiling — The upper limit of an ability measured by a test.

Concurrent validity — A measure of validity based on test scores and criterion scores that are obtained at or about the same time.

Construct validity — A relation between a test or other predictor and a theory that has been demonstrated on both logical and empirical grounds.

Content validity — The extent to which the predictors involved in a test component can be logically justified in terms of the purpose of the test.

Correlation — The relation between two variables usually expressed in the form of a correlation coefficient. Correlation deals with the degree to which two or more variables share a common variation of scores.

Correlation coefficient — Any measure of the relation between two variables; also called coefficient of correlation.

Criterion — Some measure of job performance which is usually supposed to be predicted by one or more predictors or variables.

Cross-validation — An attempt to replicate the relationships inferred from a particular study on a second group of subjects. Technically, cross-validation refers to the acquisition of a significant multiple correlation on a second sample based on a regression formula obtained in the first sample.

Cumulative frequency — The sum of all scores below the upper limit or above the lower limit of any score or class interval. Cumulative frequencies are computed by successively adding simple frequencies.

Cumulative frequency distribution — A table of the frequencies of a series of scores. It shows (1) the number of cases in all classes lower than the upper limit of each class interval or (2) the number of cases in all classes higher than the lower limit of each class interval.

Cumulative percentage — A cumulative frequency expressed as a percentage of the total number of cases.

Decile — A name given to every tenth percentile. The tenth percentile is the first decile, the twentieth percentile is the second decile, etc.

Dependent variable — The variable being observed as the independent variable or the variable under the control of the experimenter is being manipulated. Typically, the dependent variable in psychometric studies is the criterion performance measure.

Derived score — A score obtained from another score or scores by statistical methods.

Deviation — A gross score minus the mean of the distribution.

Diagnostic test — A test designed to reflect fundamental factors of performance which, when known, may suggest specific lines of remedial action.

Differential validity — Differences in criterion-related validity for separate subgroups of applicants. For example, differential validity would be said to exist if a test has different validities for younger people and older people or men and women, or blacks and whites.

Difficulty of a test item — Is reflected in the percentage of a group who pass the item.

Discriminative power of a test item — The extent to which an item is correctly answered more frequently by a group that did well on the test versus that portion of the sample that did very poorly on the test item.

Double-entry table — A two-dimensional chart in which the number in each cell shows the number of cases having X and Y scores corresponding to that cell. Same as scatter diagram.

Empirical validity — Empirically demonstrated relationship between a test and a criterion. The extent to which a test is empirically shown to perform the task assigned to it.

Employment parity — Condition which exists when a proportion of affirmative action or protected groups in the external labor market is equivalent to the proportion in the company work force without reference to classification.

Employment process — Under Title VII, the employment processing includes recruitment, application, hiring, job placement, testing, interview, compensation, promotion, transfer, termination, shift assignments, geographical and departmental assignments, and all other such activities.

Equivalent forms — Two tests that are so similar that they can be used interchangeably. Equivalent forms must test the same functions and yield the same type of score distribution, the same central tendency, and the same dispersion. Also referred to as alternate forms, comparable forms, and parallel forms.

Error of estimate — The difference between the actual value of a criterion score and that estimated by means of a regression equation.

Error of measurement — The difference between an obtained score and the corresponding true score.

Expectancy chart — A double-entry table in which the entries in each roll (or column) are expressed as percentages of the total row frequency; a table that gives the probabilities of various scores on one variable for persons with various scores on a second variable.

Expert witness — Qualified by credentials to give opinion testimony. Although this term has to be limited to a specific application in general and test validation, at least a master's degree in psychology and experience in the field is required.

Face validity — Apparent relevance of the predictor component to what the test is supposed to measure.

Factor — Any trait or quality considered in an investigation.

Factor analysis — Involves a statistical procedure which analyzes the interrelationships among a set of variables and thereby provides the proportion of the variance of each variable that is associated with each of the remaining variables.

Frequency — The number of cases falling at any score, within any class of scores, or in any specific cell.

Frequency distribution — A tabulation of the frequencies of different scores or groups of scores when they are arranged in order of magnitude.

Frequency polygon — A graphic representation of a frequency distribution in which each frequency is plotted as an ordinate value over the midpoint of its class interval and the plotted points are connected by straight lines.

G.E.D. — General equivalency degree. A G.E.D. certificate is the high school equivalency certificate which is generally recognized as equal to the high school diploma.

Histogram — A graphic representation of a frequency distribution, consisting of a series of rectangles of width equal to the size of the class interval and heights equal to the frequencies in the class intervals. Sometimes the vertical lines that separate the successive rectangles are omitted.

Independent variable — A variable under the control of the experimenter and usually used to predict or estimate another variable called the dependent variable.

Intelligence — Generally defined as the ability to learn or benefit from experience.

Intelligence quotient (IQ) — The ratio of mental age (as indicated by some test) to chronological age multiplied by 100. A deviation IQ is a variation of a standard score with the mean for any age being 100 and the standard deviation usually 15.

Internal consistency — A measure that refers to the degree to which items within a predictor component or test all measure the same quality. This phrase is often used in conjunction with the term reliability. However, the latter is somewhat broader than just internal consistency.

Inventory — This term is usually applied to interest, attitude, and personality instruments in which there is no right answer. The responses are "right" only if they are honestly given and reflect the individual's own characteristics. Less frequently, the term is used to describe a battery of ability or achievement measures designed to reflect a wide variety of skills.

IQ — Symbol for intelligence quotient.

Item analysis — Any statistical process involving the determination of the relationship between a given item and total test results which usually includes any difficulty index or the percentage of the people taking the test who got that specific item right and a discrimination index which basically identifies the degree to which high test performers did well on the item as opposed to low test performers.

Item distractor — In a multiple choice test, the alternatives include one which is a correct answer and three or four others which are not correct. These noncorrect alternatives are called distractors.

Kuder-Richardson formulas — A series of formulas for estimating the reliability of a test. The particular one to be used depends on the amount of data available or the precision of the estimate desired.

Kurtosis — The relation between the height of a curve in the region of the mode and its width as compared with that of a normal curve; the relative flatness or peakedness of a curve in the region of the mode as compared with the normal curve.

Leptokurtic — A word describing a distribution curve, it refers to the curve which is more peaked than the normal curve.

Linear — Capable of satisfactory representation by a straight line; also called straightline and rectilinear.

Linear correlation — A correlation in which the regression line is a straight line, so that for any change in the magnitude of one variable there will be a proportional change in the magnitude of the other variable. Also called rectilinear correlation.

Mean — Sum of all the scores in the sample divided by the number of scores.

Measure of central tendency — A value near the center of a frequency distribution that in some way represents the entire group of scores. Measures of central tendency include the mean, the median, and the mode. Same as the average.

Measure of dispersion — A class of measures including the range and standard deviation which reflect the degree to which scores in the distribution are spread out or constricted.

Measures of variability — Same as measure of dispersion.

Median — The point or score value that divides the cases in the distribution evenly into an upper and lower 50 percent.

Mode — The score with the highest frequency.

Multiple correlation coefficient — A number indicating the degree of relationship between a combination of variables or predictors, which are so weighted as to make the correlation a maximum, and another variable usually the criterion.

Multiple regression equation — An equation for predicting one variable from a combination of several additional variables or predictors. Each predictor is weighted so as to yield the maximum correlation with the variables to be predicted (usually the criterion).

Negative skewness — A condition of a distribution curve in which the tail of the curve is directed toward the negative side of the scale while there is a piling up of cases at the higher scores.

Norm — A type of measure based on a specified sample and used in the interpretation of raw scores.

Norm group — This is a specified sample on which the norm is based. For example, a raw score of 115 on a promotional test may be translated into a score that indicates that that score is above 75 percent of all the candidates taking the test. The norm group in this case would be all the candidates taking the test.

Normal probability curve — This is a mathematical function which most distribution of scores approximate. It is in the shape of a bell representing the fact that most scores are in the middle and the frequency of scores tend to reduce as you move away in either direction. For example, most people's IQs are around 100, certainly between 85 and 115. As you move higher than 115 or lower than 85, the number of people having those scores become fewer and fewer so that the height of the curve becomes correspondingly lower and lower.

Objective test — Any test with a definite key; that is, any test in which the judgment of the person scoring it does not enter into the score earned. These are usually multiple-choice tests.

Ogive — Same as cumulative frequency graph.

Omnibus test — Usually applied to tests of general intelligence that include questions representing many different tasks or areas of learning. The term spiral omnibus is applied to such a test when the questions are arranged in order of increasing difficulty.

Parallel forms — Same as equivalent forms.

Partial correlation coefficient — A measure of the relationship between two variables when the effects of a third variable are suspended. For example, one might be interested in taking a strong correlation between test scores and job performance and asking the question, "I wonder what would happen if we could suspend the effects of age on the correlation because it is possible that part of our result is due simply to the fact that older officers do more poorly on the tests?" The partial correlation procedure can allow us to see the amount of correlation between test scores and job performance with the effects of age suspended.

Pearson product-moment correlation coefficient — Symbolized by (r), it is a number between the values of −1 and +1 that expresses the degree of relationship between two variables. It is one of the more commonly used methods of measuring correlation.

Percentile — This is not synonymous with percentage but is the point of frequency distribution below which occur the percentage of the cases indicated by the particular percentile. Thus, 73 percent of the cases in the distribution fall below the 73rd percentile.

Performance test — A test which measures the traits, attitudes, or characteristic modes of reaction of an individual. These types of tests usually require interpretation by a psychologist.

Platykurtic — Applied to a distribution of scores whose peak is not as high as the usual normal curve. It is flatter and lower and the opposite of leptokurtic.

Point biserial correlation coefficient — A measure of correlation between two variables. One of the variables falls into many categories with the other falling into only two categories. For example, the correlation between sex and test performance.

Population — The total group about which statements are being made. This term is in contrast to the term "sample" which is a selected group or section of the overall population.

Positive skewness — Characteristic of a frequency distribution in which the tail of the distribution trails into the high end of the scale and the majority of the cases are piled up at the lower end of the scale.

Power test — A test in which the performance is determined more by ability than by speed of response. The test usually has no time limit or has sufficient time limit to allow essentially all tests takers to respond to all items. This is the reverse of what is referred to as a speed test.

Predictive validity — Extent to which scores on tests predict scores on a future criterion measure. It is expressed in the form of a correlation coefficient between the test and the criterion.

Projective technique — A test usually measuring personality and involving an ambiguous content such as inkblots, pictures, or incomplete sentences which are designed to allow the individual to project his personality into the test situations. Its usefulness has been difficult to establish by conventional reliability and validity procedures.

Quartile — Every twenty-fifth percentile. The first quartile is the twenty-fifth percentile, the second quartile is the fiftieth percentile, etc.

Random sample — A limited number of cases picked from a universal population in such a way that every individual case has an equal and independent chance of being included.

Range — The difference between the highest and lowest score obtained in the distribution. This is one of the quickest but crudest measures of variability.

Raw score — A test score as originally obtained, before any transmutation or statistical treatment.

Reliability — The consistency with which a selection component or test measures whatever it is measuring over the same sample of people. This can be done by contrasting the group's performance in one part of the test versus the second part of the test (split-half reliability) or the performance of a group on a test at time A versus its performance at time B (test re-test reliability).

Reliability coefficient — A value which varies from -1 to $+1$ reflecting the reliability of the test.

Representative sample — A sample that represents the characteristics of the population in all respects that are likely to influence results based on the sample.

Sample — A proportion of the population on whom measures of one type or another are acquired.

Scaled score — Score derived from raw scores designed to reflect certain characteristics not apparent in the raw scores. Examples are stanines, standard scores, grade equivalents.

Scatter diagram — A two-dimensional chart in which a tally mark is entered for each case in the cell at the intersection of the column and row corresponding to the X and Y scores of that case.

Scorer reliability — The degree to which different scorers agree among themselves regarding the score of a test if it is not objectively scored.

Selection ratio — The ratio of jobs to applicants. When the ratio is high, say 1 to 3, usually the cut-off for selection has to be lower than when the ratio is low, say 1 to 25.

Sigma — Theoretically, a measure of the dispersion of scores around the mean of a **population** of scores. Its counterpart, the standard deviation, is the same measure when dealing with a sample of scores.

Significant difference — An obtained difference between two sets of observations large enough so that it would have occurred rarely by chance. For example, a difference significant at the 1 percent level is one that would happen fewer than 1 times out of 100 as a result of chance variation.

Skew — Said of a distribution curve, not symmetrical.

Spearman-Broawn prophecy formula — A method for estimating the reliability of a test if it were to be lengthened by adding a certain number of equivalent items.

Speed test — A test in which the items are relatively simple. The result is that the higher scorers are people who can work faster.

Split-half reliability — A method of computing the reliability of a test using one administration and splitting the test in half, usually odd and even numbers. The scores on the two halves are then correlated one with the other.

Standard deviation (SD) — The most commonly used measure of variability obtained by dividing the difference between the raw score and the mean by the square root of the number of the cases in the sample.

Standard error of estimate — This term refers to the standard deviation of the differences between the actual values of the criterion score and that estimated from a regression equation. In other words, it is the standard deviation of the errors of estimate.

Standard score (Z) — One of a variety of standardized scores; Z score is computed by dividing the difference of the raw score and the mean of the distribution by the distribution's standard deviation. The mean of the Z score distribution is zero and the standard deviation is one. One of the major functions of the standard score is to enable comparisons of scores in different distributions.

Standardization — The systematic test development and subsequent administration to a defined sample of the population. This procedure allows the development of norms and the collection of other data essential for a detailed description of test characteristics.

Standardized test — A test that has undergone the standardization process.

Stanine — A scale which divides the distribution into nine components with a mean of five and a standard deviation of approximately two.

Statistic — A computed value such as the standard deviation that applies to a particular sample.

Stratified sample — A sample chosen by dividing a large group into smaller subgroups on the basis of characteristics likely to affect the results (e.g. age and educational class) and (2) taking a proportional number of cases from each subgroup.

Subjective test — A test for which the score depends partly on the judgment of the person who scores it.

Summation — Summation of the scores to which the term is applied; adding all the scores.

Temporal reliability — A measure of reliability which reflects the stability of scores over time, measured by a test re-test correlation.

Test re-test correlation — An estimate of the reliability coefficient obtained by correlating scores on two administrations of the same test to the same group of people.

True score — The value of a score or statistical measure in the universal population under consideration.

T score — Another standardized score similar to the Z score except that the mean of the T score distribution is fifty and the standard deviation is ten. Its use is appropriate when trying to combine scores from different distributions and when negative numbers are not desirable.

Universe — All of the cases in the class of things being investigated by statistical methods, synonymous with population. For example, the universe might contain all college graduates getting their degrees in 1976 or all females earning more than $12,000 a year.

Validity — Extent to which a test or other variable measures what it is supposed to measure. There are numerous ways of measuring validity. (See content validity, construct validity, criterion-related validity, predictive validity, face validity.)

Validity coefficient — A correlation coefficient between a test or tests and a criterion that is intended to predict.

Variability — The dispersion of the scores of a distribution from the mean or some other measure of central tendency.

Variable — Synonomous to dimension or quality, anything that can have different numerical values in different individual cases. Examples are IQ, income level, educational background, and annual salary.

Variance — A measure of variability equal to the square of the standard deviation.

Work sample test — A test involving performance like that required in a specific job. For example, having a secretary type as part of the selection for a secretarial position or a keypunch operator perform keypunching for a position.

Z score — Same as standard score, the distribution of Z scores has zero as its mean and one as its standard deviation. It permits combination of scores from different distributions.

BIBLIOGRAPHY

American Psychological Association: *Standards for Educational and Psychological Tests.* Washington, D.C., American Psychological Association, 1974.

Bray, D.W.: The management progress study. *American Psychologist, 19:* 419, 1964.

Buel, W.D.: Voluntary female clerical turnovers: The concurrent and predictive validity of a weighted application blank. *Journal of Applied Psychology, 48:*180, 1964.

Buros, O.K.: *The Seventh Mental Measurements Yearbook.* New Jersey, Gryphon Press, 1972.

Byham, W.C.: Assessment centers for spotting future managers. *Harvard Business Review, 48*(4):150, 1970.

Dunnette, M.D. and Motowidlo, S.J.: *Police Selection and Career Assessment.* Washington, D.C., National Institute of Law Enforcement and Criminal Justice, United States Department of Justice, 1976.

Equal Employment Opportunity Commission: Guidelines on employment selection procedures. *Federal Register, 35*(149):48, 1970.

Equal Employment Opportunity Coordinating Council: Guidelines on selection procedures. *Federal Register, 41*(227), 1973.

Federal Executive Agency: Employee selection guidelines — procedures, principles, and standards of conduct. *Federal Register, 41*(227), 1976.

Flanagan, J.C.: *The Performance Record for Hourly Employees.* Chicago, Science Research Associates, 1953.

Glennon, J.R.; Albright, L.E.; and Owens, W.A.: *A Catalogue of Life History Items.* Washington, D.C., American Psychological Association, 1966.

Guion, R.M.: *Personnel Testing.* New York, McGraw-Hill, 1965.

Kerner, O.: *The Kerner Commission Report.* Washington, D.C., United States Department of Justice, 1967.

Lawshe, C.H.: A quantitative approach to content validity. *Personnel Psychology, 28:*563, 1975.

McCann, F.: Physical fitness tests. In Donovan, J.J.: *Recruitment and Selection in the Public Service.* Chicago, International Personnel Management Association, 1967.

McCarthy, W.; Davis, C.P. III; Lundquist, D.G.; Lookingbill, D.L.; O'Leary, R.C.; and Menne, J.: *Job Analysis Guidelines.* Des Moines, Iowa Merit Employment Department, 1974.

McCarthy, W.; Davis, C.P. III; Lundquist, D.G.; Lookingbill, D.L.; O'Leary,

R.C.; Kroon, B.A.; and Menne, J.: *Job Analysis Questionnaire for Selection Device Content Validity*, 2nd ed. Des Moines, Iowa Merit Employment Department, 1977.

McClelland, D.: Testing for competence rather than for intelligence. *American Psychologist, 28:*1, 1973.

McCormick, E.: *A Study of Job Characteristics and Job Dimensions, Based on the Position Analysis Questionnaire.* Lafayette, Indiana, Occupational Research Center at Purdue University, 1969.

O'Leary, L.R.: Fair employment, job relatedness and sound psychometric practice; a dilemma and a partial solution. *American Psychologist, 28:* 147, 1973.

O'Leary, L.R.: Is employment testing a thing of the past? *Personnel Journal, 5:*13, 1972.

O'Leary, L.R.: Objectivity bias and job relatedness: Can we have our cake and eat it too? *Public Personnel Management,* 423, November–December, 1976a.

O'Leary, L.R.: *Interviewing For the Decisionmaker.* Chicago, Nelson-Hall, 1976b.

Primoff, Ernest: *How to Prepare and Conduct Job Element Examinations.* Washington, D.C., United States Civil Service Commission, 1974.

"Student" (W.S. Gosset): The probable error of a mean *Biometrika, 6:*1, 1908.

Tyler, Leona E.: *Tests and Measurements.* Englewood Cliffs, Prentice-Hall, 1963.

United States Department of Labor: *Handbook for Analyzing Jobs.* Washington, D.C., United States Department of Labor, 1972.

INDEX